SATISFIED...

At Last!

Learning to be Fully Satisfied with the Bread of Life

Kay Harms

WestBow
PRESS
A DIVISION OF THOMAS NELSON
& ZONDERVAN

Scripture quotations taken from the New American Standard Bible®,Copyright © 1960, 1962, 1963, 1968, 1971, 1972, 1973, 1975, 1977, 1995 by The Lockman Foundation Used by permission. (www.Lockman.org)

WestBow Press books may be ordered through booksellers or by contacting:

WestBow Press
A Division of Thomas Nelson & Zondervan
1663 Liberty Drive
Bloomington, IN 47403
www.westbowpress.com
1 (866) 928-1240

Because of the dynamic nature of the Internet, any web addresses or links contained in this book may have changed since publication and may no longer be valid. The views expressed in this work are solely those of the author and do not necessarily reflect the views of the publisher, and the publisher hereby disclaims any responsibility for them.

Any people depicted in stock imagery provided by Thinkstock are models, and such images are being used for illustrative purposes only. Certain stock imagery © Thinkstock.

ISBN: 978-1-4908-9156-9 (sc)
ISBN: 978-1-4908-9157-6 (e)

Library of Congress Control Number: 2015914062

Print information available on the last page.

WestBow Press rev. date: 08/18/2015

To my husband,
James…

For years I loaded the burden of my fulfillment and joy on your shoulders but, as broad and strong as they may be, you were not meant to carry that responsibility. You have been a good husband, a responsible provider for our family, a trustworthy friend, a constant encourager, and a loving father. You have been exactly what God meant for you to be to me. You and I have complemented each other well. We have enjoyed the gift of marriage, the joy of parenthood, and the journey of ministry together and loved every minute. But you were never meant to be my all-in-all.

Through your ministry and in our relationship, you have pointed to Jesus as the all sufficient Savior. Your personal walk with the Lord has consistently illustrated that He alone can satisfy our every need. We have depended on Him to provide financially, to give wisdom, to direct our steps, to buffer our falls, and to grant us daily grace. I know He is your best friend and He's mine too. That mutual friendship and the triangle it forms have kept us united and on each other's team even when we were at odds. What a blessing to know that when you and I go tell our Best Friend on each other, we're talking to the same Friend!

Thank you for doing this ministry thing with me. I love you.

Kay

Acknowledgments

I would like to express my deepest appreciation to those who have encouraged and assisted me as I've written this study. I will not begin to name names for fear of leaving someone out who prayed for me, spoke an encouraging word to me, asked repeatedly when I would be done, or even helped fund my efforts. But suffice it to say that without the constant nudges in the right direction these words might just be another file on my computer instead of a book in the hands of hungry Bible students. Thank you, dear friends and family members, for pushing me toward my goal with unflappable love and support.

I am indebted to two special women in particular, however. Kim Tucker delved into this Bible study and looked up every scripture, answered every question and even drew every requested diagram as I wrote it. She was my gracious guinea pig and for her willingness to do this Bible study while she juggled several others she was teaching, I owe her a debt of gratitude. Trudie Jackson graciously gave of her time and energy to edit my work. I deeply appreciate her diligence and partnership in ministry through this unglamorous but necessary task. Thank you, ladies.

Contents

Foreword

I am thrilled you have chosen to join me for a Bible study. I want you to know I have not taken the writing of this study lightly for even one minute. I consider it a great privilege and an even greater responsibility to carefully lead you in a study of God's precious and inspired Word.

I am not a great theologian. I am simply a student of the Bible who has found a great treasure worth sharing. Please feel free to question my statements and my interpretation of scripture. It is my hope to lead you into the depths of God's Word so that you can read its truth for yourself, claiming it as your own, and pressing it into your heart so that it makes its indelible imprint. My words are nothing special, but His surely are.

Satisfied…at Last is such a personal message to me. Even as a good Sunday school student who had her daily quiet time, I struggled for years to find contentment. I just knew there was something missing. I had no doubt I was a true believer and was certain the Holy Spirit lived in me; however, I continued to search outside of my faith for that which would satisfy my soul.

I first realized I had a problem when my neediness and demanding spirit began to create a wedge between my husband and me. I couldn't understand why he wasn't meeting all of my needs. Wasn't he supposed to? But, alas, no matter how hard he tried (and he did try) he couldn't.

Through the years I have sought satisfaction for my hungry soul in any number of venues. Some proved to be disappointing right from the get-go. Others provided satisfaction, but it was fleeting and unpredictable. A few turned out to be dangerous and still others made me a fool. Finally, I found that the only source of true satisfaction comes from Jesus, the self-proclaimed Bread of Life. He alone can meet my every need and does so willingly and with such grace and dignity. He never makes a fool out of me.

I wrote this Bible study because I have seen that familiar "woman-on-a-hunt-for-satisfaction" look on too many faces. I hear their stories and their frustrations and I sense they are looking to their husbands, children, professions, and friends to meet their souls' desires. I have talked with women who honestly believe that if they only lived in a different neighborhood, had a better wardrobe, worked for a more appreciative boss, or earned another degree, they would finally be content. And I hear young women just starting out in life who are mapping out their treasure hunt for satisfaction as though their five-year plan for college, career and marriage will result in complete bliss with never another worry.

Dear friend, are you hungry? Do you ever wake up and just have a nagging longing for what you do not know? Do you sometimes look around and wonder, "Is this it? Is there more?" Do you find yourself frustrated with the people in your life because they don't give you the time you need or the attention you deserve? Do you accumulate possessions with the hope they will give you some sense of joy only to later find them both bothersome and outdated? Do you engage in one pursuit after another, believing that surely this activity will be the one that really rocks your world, ignites your flame? I've done all those things.

I'm going to cheat and tell you one of the most delightful things you'll learn in this study. God knows you're hungry. In fact, He made you that way and is more than willing to satisfy that soul hunger single-handedly…and He is up to the task.

And so I invite you to join me on this journey to contentment. I can honestly tell you that I am satisfied, completely satisfied, at last. You can be too.

"Come and hear, all who fear God, and I will tell you what He has done for my soul." (Psalm 66:16)

Week 1 - Are You Hungry?

Why is it that sometimes we feel perfectly on top of the world and at other times we feel, for no particular reason, like the world is on top of us?

I've noticed that my behavior and emotions often change depending upon how "full" or "empty" I am. You know those sensations. You feel full when you believe life is good, all your needs are being met, your relationships are meaningful and intact, your work is satisfying, and your days are productive. Or maybe you feel empty when no one seems to notice or appreciate you, your work has become drudgery, you've lost your sense of purpose, you're bored with your same old furniture and wardrobe, or you just…feel…disconnected…from the universe.

Often our emotions, thoughts, dispositions and behaviors ebb and flow in correlation to the fullness level of our tank. What tank? That internal space that longs to be filled with something good and satisfying. Just as our appetites for various foods change, so do our desires to be filled with different things. Sometimes we need a little love, sometimes we want appreciation, and other times our lives need purpose, and so on and so on. The bottom line is we're yearning for something to make us feel whole and alive. And when that yearning goes unmet, the disappointment usually shows up in our tone of voice, on our faces, and in the little things we do.

This week we'll discover what Jesus has to say about the hungers of our souls. We'll do a little self-examination to better understand what it is we're longing for. Finally, we'll discover where and how we can get those hungers met. If you're hungry for anything at all, you've come to the right place. I invite you to take a seat at the table, put your napkin in your lap, and prepare for a feast. Indeed, there is one who can satisfy your soul. Let's meet Him and find out how.

Day 1
We All Like to Eat

I'm so glad it is acceptable these days to admit you love food. I am, unashamedly, a foodie! I love to go to new restaurants, try different foods, and explore exotic flavors. I enjoy swapping recipes with good cooks, watching the experts whip up a savory dish on The Food Network, buying new cooking supplies at hen parties, and experimenting with new ingredients when cooking for my family. Not yet convinced that I'm more into food than the average American housewife? How about this? I even enjoy grocery shopping – to the point that I have to *make* myself head for the check-out line.

Most people enjoy food on some level. Even if you're somebody who eats from a very narrow menu – perhaps a vegetarian, a diabetic, or just a picky eater – you probably enjoy the benefits of delicious and satisfying food. There's just something satisfying about sitting down to a well prepared, aromatic, and tasty meal, savoring each bite, and leaving the table pleasantly full and nourished for the next portion of your day.

Wondering where I'm going with this? Perhaps this is a strange place to begin a Bible study, but as we ease ourselves into this topical study let's start with a few fun and simple questions.

What are some of your favorite foods?

1

Describe an exceptionally satisfying meal you consumed recently. What made it good? Where did you eat the meal and with whom did you share it? Note anything that made it special.

Now that I've managed to awaken your taste buds and set your stomach to growling, let's open God's Word and read through a passage we will be feasting on throughout the week. In an attempt to draw some precepts from John 6 that we can apply to our lives, we are going to study the passage *inductively*. That means we will:

- slow down and read with a purpose
- allow the text to speak for itself
- ask questions such as *who, what, where, when, why,* and *how* as we read
- follow careful observation with responsible interpretation
- apply what we learn to our lives

In order to fully absorb what you are reading, I encourage you to consider marking in your Bible as you read. It's amazing what a few colored pencils can do to help you better understand the complexities of God's Word. Sweet friend, don't be afraid to mark in your Bible. Visualize the well placed underlines and circles as the forks and knives that help you ingest the meat of God's Word.

In fact you will probably find those marks to be a treasure to you as the years go by and as you return to those passages to dine again and again. If you're willing to make a few carefully selected marks in your Bible, I'll guide you in choosing what to mark and how to mark it. If you still prefer not to mark in your Bible, I suggest you print a copy of our selected passage from an Internet source such as www.Biblegateway.com so you can mark it instead.

We are going to read a small portion of John 6 several times today. Please don't be tempted, as I often am, to take a short cut and read it only once. Reading a passage several times and looking for different information each time is foundational to studying the Bible inductively. This practice is what allows the Holy Spirit time to open your eyes to the most subtle brushstrokes which ultimately make the picture come together into a powerful, life-changing image.

Please pause to pray, asking the Holy Spirit to direct your study and open your eyes to His teaching.

_____ I stopped to pray before proceeding with today's Bible study.

Please read John 6:1-14, marking the following words and their synonyms as you go:

Jesus	I like to mark all references to Jesus in red. I put a small red cross above His name and the pronouns referring to Him.
multitude	I marked any reference to the multitude in orange (people, men, everyone, etc.)

Now, based on what you read, answer the following questions.
Where is Jesus?

What has He been doing according to verse 2?

What is Jesus' concern in verse 5?

Please read John 6:1-14 again, this time marking all references to *time* and *amounts*.
For instance, you might put a small clock like this ☺ to mark a reference to *time* in verse 4. I used the pound sign, #, to mark references to *amount* as in verse 7 (I found two here). Remember to slow down a little!

Based on what you read, answer these questions:
When do the events of chapter 6 take place?

Who answered Jesus' question about where they could buy food by telling Him about amounts?

Think with me on this one. What specifically did Jesus ask the disciples in verse 5?

As I mentioned earlier, we're studying the scripture today by asking the questions *who, what, when, where, why* and *how*. These are the very same questions I learned to ask while attending journalism school and had the task of writing news articles. When asking questions in an interview you want to make sure you get correlating answers. When you ask a *where* question, you need a *where* answer. And if you ask *who*, you don't want a *why* answer. You probably noticed that Jesus asked one of these questions of His disciples. He asked them *where* they could buy bread to feed the multitude. Look at the two answers the disciples gave Jesus in verses 7 and 9. Did they answer the question *where* or did they answer the wrong question?

How would you classify their answers? What question(s) were they seemingly answering?
Circle one or two.   Who?   What?   When?   How?   Why?   Where?

Bless their hearts; the disciples were still learning how to respond to Jesus. Perhaps you and I are still on the same journey. I think it's noteworthy that Jesus didn't seem to get frustrated with Philip and Andrew for answering His *where* question with *how* and *who* answers. Instead, I imagine He smiled at them with compassion before He went on to answer the question Himself. You see, the answer He was looking for, I believe, was *nowhere*. There is nowhere we can go to get enough food to fill these people, Lord, except to You. And so, since His disciples seemed confused by the question and unable to supply the correct answer, Jesus simply sat the people down and began feeding them. He *showed* them the answer to His question.

One last time, please read John 6:1-14 in your Bible. This time look for and mark references to the following words and their synonyms:

eat	I marked words like *eat* and *ate* with a brown box around the word.
food, bread, fish	I marked these words and their pronouns by underlining them in brown.
fill	I marked *fill* and *filled* by drawing a brown circle around the word and lightly shading it in.

You've done a lot of work today. But I don't want us to finish this session having exerted our brain muscles but wondering what the benefit was. Let's answer just a few more questions based on our reading and then we'll be ready to draw some basic conclusions from our study.

Who initiated the marvelous mealtime we read about in John 6? Whose idea was it to fill the people's bellies? Explain your answer.

How full do you think the people were when the meal was over? Why?

What was the people's reaction to the meal Jesus supplied?

Like I mentioned earlier, I'm thrilled that it is considered "in" to admit your passion for food these days. I don't have to be a closet foodie! The more exciting news is that Jesus recognizes our affinity for food as well. He wasn't annoyed by the fact that 5,000+ people were hungry for something to put in their stomachs via their salivating mouths. And if he heard a few stomachs growl while he taught the people deep and eternal lessons, He evidently didn't sigh with impatience or disgust. In fact, Jesus is the one who took it upon Himself to feed each and every person gathered on that hilltop beside the Sea of Galilee. He didn't simply announce, "Time for a dinner break! You have a selection of fast food restaurants to choose from down the road. Meet back here in one hour." No, He sat them down, said the blessing, and provided 12 gentlemen waiters to serve them a hearty meal of fish and bread.

Ok, so it was a fast, convenient and free meal, but was it filling? You betcha! If my family and I are any representation of human nature at all, I can guarantee you those people didn't just politely take a small portion from those laden baskets. They were hungry and food was multiplying before their eyes. My guess is that more than a few people went to bed with belly aches that night. And just in case the readers of this gospel account wondered if the people were given an ample meal or just a snack to tide them over, Jesus instructed the disciples to gather the leftovers *after* the people were completely full. Each of the twelve men gathered a basket full of extra food.

Here are some very basic truths we can responsibly pull from today's lesson even before going any further in our study. Tuck these away for future exploration. While we may be talking about physical food that feeds the belly today, in the coming days we will be moving on to other kinds of food that satisfies a different hunger. Examine these truths and see if they ring with multiple meanings.

1. Everyone gets hungry. It's natural, normal and healthy to hunger.
2. Jesus willingly and lovingly acknowledges our hunger. He is not impatient with it or put off by it.
3. Jesus is able to satisfy hunger creatively, completely, and single-handedly. You can sit down and take a load off while He whips up something satisfying and sufficient.

Day 2
What Are You Hungry For?

If you remembered that we spent most of the previous lesson talking about how Jesus satisfied the multitude's physical hunger with bounteous fish and bread, you may have thought ahead today and prepared yourself a snack to munch on while studying, just in case. But while your stomach may have growled as we read John 6:1-14 over and over yesterday, I'm hoping to awaken your senses to a different kind of appetite as we continue on in the same chapter today.

Jesus was a masterful teacher. He knew that it would take more than skillful teaching to get people to think about spiritual concepts, matters of the heart, and eternal consequences when their minds are so firmly fixed on their current physical needs. Jesus wisely stopped teaching long enough to silence the crowds' growling stomachs so they could focus on what he had to say. He also realized that by positively addressing a common physical dilemma he could then help his audience relate to a common spiritual need which they had probably yet to identify themselves. They knew they were hungry for food, but did they know they had other hungers as well? Did you know that you hunger for more than food too? In our age of pop psychology and afternoon talk show sociology, you probably were aware that we all long for many things with the same urgency that our bellies ache for food. But what exactly are you hungry for? That's what we are going to explore in this lesson.

Please pause to pray, asking the Holy Spirit to direct your study and open your eyes to His teaching.

_____ I stopped to pray before proceeding with today's Bible study.

Please read John 6:15-21 marking all references to *Jesus* and the *multitude* in the same ways you did in the previous lesson.

Please read the passage again, marking any references to *time* and *amounts* in the same manner you used previously.

Briefly describe the activity of Jesus and His disciples during the night following the feeding of the multitude.

At the break of the next day, where are Jesus and His disciples?

Now, let's move along and catch up with Jesus in the next passage. Please read John 6:22-27 marking all references to *Jesus* and the *multitude*. Also mark references to *time*.

Describe the multitude's reaction to Jesus' overnight disappearance. From their actions and words in this passage, how would you describe the atmosphere of the group?

Read John 6:22-27 again marking all references to *eating*, *food* (*bread, loaves*), and *filled*.

Jesus identifies two types of food in verse 27. What are they?

1. Food which ...
2. Food which ...

Obviously, when Jesus mentions food that endures to eternal life He is not talking about frozen dinners or canned vegetables. My husband cleaned out my pantry and refrigerator while I was out of town recently and subsequently accused me of trying to keep some outdated items until the rapture, but I don't think Jesus had my three-year-old salad dressings in mind. He was referring to a food that not only lasted into eternity, but one that also satisfied hungers of an eternal nature. This is the point at which Jesus takes the discussion about food to a different level. He is no longer talking about grumbling tummies and salivating mouths. And He's no longer offering fish and bread.

Jesus had been performing miracles and healing people to the crowd's amazement. Now that He had a captive audience, He longed to help them understand who He really was and what He ultimately came to offer them. It was time to discuss spiritual issues. It would take the crowd a little longer to catch on to what He was talking about, and some of them never did. Hopefully you and I are aware that Jesus was addressing the soul hungers that each of us feels deep within our beings. The same God who had sensed and acknowledged their physical hunger was now demonstrating His awareness of and His answer to their longings of the soul.

From our previous lesson we concluded that it is natural, normal and healthy to hunger. While we may have drawn that conclusion from an episode concerning physical food, the same is true of soul hungers. God created us with an appetite for certain things. Though psychologists and sociologists have tried through the years to specify the basic needs of humans, their attempts to define and categorize human longings will continue to fall short if they do not acknowledge the God who created us with those hungers. You and I do not need to be psycho-analyzed in order to know that we indeed long for certain things. In fact, we all have numerous longings. Some of them drive us more than others (more on that later), but we all share the desire for "more."

Why do you think God created us with longings, desires, or hungers? (Read Psalm 107:6-9 for a clue.)

Maybe your answer included the fact that it is our longings that should drive us to our creator. Just like the desires for food, warmth, attention and comfort cause a newborn baby to cry out for its mother, our soul hungers are meant to initiate within us a search and longing for our Father. When that newborn finds his desires to be fulfilled by his mother, a mutually satisfying and loving relationship is formed between the child and its parent. Likewise, when our hungers are satisfied by our Father – and they all can be – we grow to love and depend on Him.

What are you hungry for? Look over the list of normal soul desires below. Consider them carefully. This is not an exhaustive list and you can add any other soul hungers you think of. After careful consideration, indicate your top 8 longings.

_____unconditional love	_____freedom
_____acceptance	_____power
_____significance	_____relationship
_____companionship	_____commitment
_____support	_____knowledge
_____security	_____self expression
_____adventure	_____intimacy with another
_____mercy	_____respect
_____purpose	_____achievement
_____family, a sense of belonging	_____rest
_____other _____	

Write the three desires you most strongly relate to in the space below. Granted, these may change tomorrow, but let's identify for now what you are most hungry for *today*.

In the event that you are having a difficult time identifying your greatest hungers, our scripture for today includes a highly reliable indicator. In fact this revealing clue is the very thing that prompted Jesus' discussion with the crowd about hungers and foods that satisfy those hungers.

Jesus indicates in John 6:26 two reasons the people have been following Him. He alludes to the fact that they *had been* following him for one reason, but now he says they have crossed the Sea of Galilee to catch up with Him for a completely different reason. Both motivating factors have caused the people to leave their homes and work and obligations to follow Him at some cost. What could be driving them to such lengths?

According to John 6:26, why *had* the people been following Jesus *before*?

Why did Jesus say they were following Him now?

According to Jesus the people were initially interested in Him because of the miracles He performed. But they are more than interested now. Their hunger for food has driven them to follow Him across the sea and into new territory. Ah, the driving power of hunger.

Our hungers drive us to great lengths as well.

- An insatiable hunger for love can drive us into the arms of someone who offers us a dose of affection.
- The desire for acceptance can drive us to compromise our own convictions in order to fit in.
- The hunger for a sense of belonging might drive a lonely and ostracized teenager to link up with a gang that promises membership privileges.
- Our desire for adventure can drive us to do risky things while throwing caution to the wind.
- The need for security might cause a young woman who grew up fatherless to attach herself to someone who can provide for her physical needs even without the promise of love.
- And a longing for achievement can drive an individual right on up the proverbial ladder, even if it means stepping on others on the way up.

In the past, some of my hungers have driven me to
- compromise my standards,
- say things I later regretted,
- work tirelessly at futile pursuits,
- place unreasonable expectations on others,
- charge up my credit card,
- and hurt those I loved.

I can certainly identify with the mob that chased Jesus down in an effort to get another meal out of Him. There have been times when the people in my life have temporarily satisfied one of my hungers and I have hounded them for more and more until they have grown frustrated and angry. I have chased people, experiences, goals, and things in order to get my fill.

What about you? What have your hungers driven you to?

I don't normally like to end a study session on such a low note, but maybe this is just where God would have us part ways today. We probably all need a little solitary time to let the weight of this lesson sink in. Sweet friend, our hungers are a force to be reckoned with and we must not shy away from being truthful about where they have taken us. I encourage you to spend some time in prayer now, asking God to show you where your hungers have driven you. But take courage. Whatever path you have gone down in an effort to try to satisfy your hungers, God is all about detours.

Day 3
What Shall We Do?

Occasionally I get such a hankering for something creamy, cheesy, and rich that I will stop what I'm doing, get out the recipe books, and actually cook something that fits the bill. And I'm not talking about cooking dinner for my family. I'm confessing to you that my hunger for warm cheese can actually drive me to get out the pots and pans at 2:00 in the afternoon. Either that or I'll get in my car and drive to Target, claiming to be running errands, but all along knowing that my real goal is a personal pan cheese pizza from the snack counter. Sick? Maybe, but my 45 years tell me that most of you have similar passions that drive you to equally extreme measures. Am I right? (By the way, I'm talking maybe once every six months. I don't want you to think this is a weekly habit! If so, I'd really need a little intervention therapy.)

In our previous lesson we discovered that, like my appetite for cheese, our soul hungers can also drive us to great lengths. Hopefully, you have had some time to prayerfully think about what you are currently hungering for and what those hungers are driving you to. If the remainder of this Bible study is going to bear any lasting fruit in our lives, we will need to get real about our hungers and the roads we have been going down to satisfy them. While I don't expect you to write confidential, harmful or humiliating information in your study book, I do suggest you write enough so you alone feel like you've put the truth on paper. The point is to get it out in the open, even if the open is just between you and God.

In the space below, write about your greatest current soul hungers and how you have been trying to satisfy those desires. Be honest and thorough without writing anything too personal.

Now let's turn to God's Word to find out how we should be getting our hungers filled correctly. Do not think for one minute, however, that we will discuss this topic exhaustively today. This is one of the topics we will spend a great amount of time and energy on in days to come. However, today we will discover that in John 6 Jesus addressed the people's misdirected attempts to satisfy their hungers through the wrong means. He also indicated where we are to go for satisfaction.

Please pause to pray, asking the Holy Spirit to direct your study and open your eyes to His teaching.

_____ I stopped to pray before proceeding with today's Bible study.

Please read John 6:26-29 in your Bible. You have already marked 26-27. Now mark any references to Jesus and the multitude in 28-29. Also mark references to God the Father in all four verses. I use a blue triangle.

As a refresher, what did the people's physical hunger cause them to do?

According to John 6:27, where does Jesus say the people can get the "food which endures to eternal life"?

Circle the words *work* and *works* with a pencil in John 6:27-29. Using whatever study tool you have access to (Expository dictionary of New Testament words, English dictionary, Internet dictionary, etc.), define the words below.

work – (vs. 27,28 – used as a verb)

work – (vs. 29 – used as a noun)

works – (vs. 28 – used as a noun)

The words *work* and *works* used in 28 and 29 as nouns are the same word: *ergon* in Greek. This word denotes "a deed or act" and in this case refers to an act of God. The word *work* used in 27 and 28 as a verb refers to a different kind of work. *Ergazomai* also has its root in *ergon*, but means to "to work something, produce, perform," as well as to "earn by working for, work for, labor." This word implies that the subject is laboring and performing in order to receive something that is highly sought after and needed, something greatly desired.

How, in verse 27, does Jesus tell the crowd they should work for the physical food that perishes?

In verse 27 Jesus tells the people *not* to work for the food which perishes, but encourages them to seek the food which endures to eternal life, the food that satisfies more than temporal hungers. Still, even though Jesus promises that the Son of Man will give them this food, He doesn't really explain how they can attain it. Like me, these people want Jesus to speak plainly to them. Exactly how do they go about getting this eternal food? And notice how they want to get it. They want to work for it. They want to know exactly what they need to do to earn this special food.

How does this attitude correspond to people's quest for spiritual food today? Do you see indications that people want to *work* for spiritual fulfillment, to *earn* God's gifts, to *labor* in order to deserve spiritual blessings?

"Okay," Jesus seems to say. "You want to work for this food? Here's the work: believe in Him whom God has sent. That's it." Of course Jesus was referring to Himself as the One sent by God. He is the one who can satisfy the people with food that does not perish. But can they work for it? No. Can they deserve it? No. Can they perform in such a way as to earn it? No. They just have to trust Him to provide all they need.

Dear friends, that is precisely where we find ourselves today. There is a food that satisfies our souls to the very core of our being. It smells divine, tastes heavenly, provides every nutrient our soul longs for, and leaves us filling satisfied and content; however, there is no way we can work for that food. We cannot dress up nicely enough or turn on the charm enough to get it from a man. We cannot labor hard enough or act smart enough to earn it from our boss. We will never bake enough cookies, help with enough science projects or bandage enough scraped knees to get it from our children. And we need not even try to serve long enough or hard enough to get it from the church. You and I need to stop working to get our fill from all the wrong places through all the wrong means. We will never succeed in doing so, and we're only frustrating ourselves and everyone we try to mooch off of for a meal.

Reminiscent of Jesus' question to His disciples in John 6:5, *where* are we to go to get our hungers satisfied?

And according to John 6:29, how do we attain this ever-satisfying food from Him?
_____ Earn it through good behavior.
_____ Believe in Him.
_____ Do works for God.
_____ Beg the people around us.

Now if you're like me, this all sounds like good Sunday school theory. You know it's the right answer, but you're a little skeptical about how it actually plays out in your life. Is simply believing in Jesus really going to somehow satisfy my every hunger? And exactly where, when, and how does this transaction take place? What does this spiritual food look like and how do I lay my hands on it? For that matter, how do I eat it? Ah. These are good questions to look into tomorrow.

$\curlyvee$

Day 4
Believe In Him

One of my favorite fast food restaurants is Chipotle Mexican Grill. They have deliciously huge burritos, salads, and "bowls" made to order. Of course Chipotle is one of those places, like Starbucks, where you have to know *how* to order. I'm sure more than one first time visitor with a shaky self-esteem has run out the door without ever ordering. It's the kind of place where the people in front of you in line can sound intimidating and other-worldly as they rattle off their orders of "I'll have a burrito with rice, black beans, barbacoa, mild salsa, sour cream and cheese. Cut it in half, please, and guacamole on the side." I'm pretty sure the first time I ate at Chipotle I asked my husband just to order for me. I was totally lost. But after eating the first few bites of my delicious burrito I knew I'd be coming back and I'd have to learn to order for myself.

As we rejoin Jesus and the hungry crowd in John 6 today, we encounter a queue of people ready to put in their order for this eternally satisfying food Jesus has offered. But, like a first time Chipotle customer, they seem a little unsure about how to make their request. Let's spend a little extra time on one key concept in John 6:29 so we can methodically build our own set of instructions for acquiring the "bread of God…which…gives life to the world."

Please pause to pray, asking the Holy Spirit to direct your study and open your eyes to His teaching.

_____ I stopped to pray before proceeding with today's Bible study.

Please read John 6:27-29 as a review and to put today's scripture in context. Underline any phrases that explain how to get the food which endures to eternal life.

How does Jesus say they can receive the food which endures to eternal life? (Check all that apply)
_____ Jesus will give it to them.
_____ Work hard to earn it.
_____ Believe in Him whom God has sent.
_____ Order it at the drive thru window.
_____ The ravens will bring it each morning.

Using whatever study aids you have available, look up the word "believe" used by Jesus in verse 29. Hint: it's the Greek word *pisteuo*. Record what you find here.

When Jesus told the hungry people who were following Him that the work of God was to "believe in Him whom He has sent," He didn't simply imply that they needed only to admit He stood before them. It wasn't enough to casually acknowledge Jesus existed or even that He was indeed the one whom God had sent. He was asking that they be fully persuaded of His claim to be the Messiah and with all that the title implied. He was asking them to put their full confidence in Him as a teacher, to rely upon Him for their eternal salvation, to depend upon Him to do the things He said He would do, and to entrust their lives to Him. In terms of our subject matter for this Bible study, He was asking them to forsake every other method of having their needs met and depend solely on Him.

John, the beloved disciple of Jesus who penned the book of John in the Bible, used the word *pisteuo*, translated *believe*, ninety-nine times, in contrast to the other writers of the Gospels who used the word nine or ten times each. To understand why John used the word so often, read John 20:30-31.

According to John 20:30-31, why does the book of John contain the particular stories about Jesus' ministry that it does?

According to John 20:31, what is the result of believing that Jesus is the Christ, the Son of God?

If believing is the key to receiving the food that satisfies the soul, perhaps we need to understand a little more about what we are to believe and the results of believing. What better place to research what it means to believe than the book of John. Let's look at a few more of the beloved disciple's ninety-nine uses of the word to get a better feel for the implications.

Read the following scriptures and note who or what Jesus claims to be in each.

John 4:25-26	Jesus claims to be...
John 5:17-18	Jesus claims to be...
John 6:48	Jesus claims to be...
John 9:5	Jesus claims to be...
John 10:9	Jesus claims to be...
John 10:11	Jesus claims to be...
John 11:25	Jesus claims to be...
John 14:6	Jesus claims to be...
John 15:5	Jesus claims to be...

These are a few of the things we are asked to believe with more than mental assent. We are to stake our very lives on these claims, live as though they are true and trustworthy, and depend on Jesus to be exactly who He says He is.

Read the following scriptures and draw lines to match each one with the corresponding *result* of *believing* in Jesus.

John 1:12	You will not be judged.
John 3:18	You will become a child of God.
John 7:38-39	You will have your thirst quenched by the Holy Spirit.
John 9:38	You will see the glory of God.
John 11:25-26	You will worship Jesus.
John 11:40	You will have life in His name.
John 12:36	You will become sons of light.
John 20:31	You will live and never die.

Look over the list above again. One at a time, carefully examine each result of belief in Jesus and notice how each one does indeed satisfy a hunger of the soul. In the space below each result, **note what soul hunger might be satisfied through believing in Him.** I'll get you started. I would note below the first result, "You will not be judged," that Jesus satisfies my hunger for *acceptance, approval,* and *forgiveness.*

The list we just worked through is not exhaustive. Obviously there are many other hungers of the soul Jesus satisfies. In fact there isn't a hunger of the soul Jesus can't satisfy. I simply wanted us to recognize that when we believe Jesus is who He says He is and we stake our lives on these beliefs, perhaps we've taken the first step in correctly placing our order for satisfying soul food.

I recently heard a sad and disturbing story about a young woman who was sexually molested as a child by a family friend. The woman, now in her early 30s, has struggled with multiple issues, such as drug addictions, credit card debt, and unhealthy relationships since her teen years. Fortunately, she is successfully dealing with each of the problems. However, this young woman continues to harbor a great deal of anger toward her childhood perpetrator. When she was in her early 20s and trying to reach out for help, she told her parents about the repeated sexual offenses of her childhood, but they did not believe her story. She became angry and detached from her parents. Later, when the young woman decided to press charges on her own against the family friend who had violated her, it was discovered that her story was indeed trustworthy and substantiated by a bounty of evidence. The parents now believed her and tried to help; however, the young lady ran into an unfortunate and unfair barrier in the legal system. Due to circumstances beyond her control, the case would never go to trial and she would never find justice for the crime that was committed against her.

The young woman craves justice. Her hunger for vengeance against her perpetrator gnaws at her like an empty stomach full of gastric juices seeking something to devour. Sadly, she has hit a roadblock and will likely never see her offender serve any time for his heinous crime. Is her desire for justice never to be satisfied? Does she simply have to learn to live with the injustice and move on? Or is there food that can fill even this seemingly hopeless hunger?

According to what we have learned from scripture today, Jesus can indeed satisfy even this young woman's hunger for revenge. He can grant her desire for justice. How? Through her belief in Him. When the young woman believes what Jesus said about her situation and entrusts it to Him, He can begin to satisfy her hunger. Granted, when our hungers are instigated and increased by wrong-doing, perversion, and injustice, as in the case of this young woman, they are not satisfied overnight. But belief is definitely the first step and the channel through which Jesus can satisfy her soul.

Let's apply what we've learned in previous days to this young woman's situation. What have her unsatisfied hungers for resolution, wholeness, justice and revenge driven her to?

Now that she realizes she has been going to the wrong places to get her fill, she still needs to find satisfaction for her hungers or she will return to her old habits or possibly find worse ones. Where can she get her hunger filled?

Read the following passages to find out what this woman needs to believe. Summarize your findings.

Matthew 18:5-7 –

John 5:25-29 –

When you visit a Chipotle Mexican Grill, the first step in ordering your meal is simply deciding if you'd like a salad, a bowl, or a burrito. You can't get a sandwich, a pizza, or a cup of soup. The intriguingly bare menu board on the wall may seem a little confusing to first time customers, but once you watch the process of adding savory meats, a variety of beans, rice, corn, salsas to fit your heat preferences, homemade guacamole or sour cream, and cheese to a bed of lettuce, a fresh tortilla or a bowl, you get the hang of how this thing works. If you are ordering to eat there, you'll need first to decide if you'd like a salad, a bowl, or a burrito. That's step one. Want to skip the first step? Then step out of the way and let the next customer place their order. Quite simply, you can't skip step one. And so it is with placing your order for soul food.

Sweet sister, many of us would say we want Jesus to supply our every heart desire, our every hunger of the soul, but we're standing at the counter confused by the menu. We've watched other Christians step away from the counter satisfied and thrilled with how Jesus has satisfied their hungers, but we're confused about how to place our own order. We study the same Bible these joy filled Christians study, go to the same churches, and read the same Christian books, but we still feel confused about just how Jesus is supposed to satisfy our every hunger. Does this thing really work? Can Jesus really feed us bread that endures to eternal life? Can He really satisfy me so I don't go searching in all the wrong places for my needs, wants, and desires? Yes, yes, and yes. But first, I must believe. Believing Jesus *is*, *can*, and *will* is like deciding if I want a salad, a bowl, or a burrito. Belief is the channel through which Jesus can feed my soul. There is no other way.

Many of us say we believe in Jesus, but we live as though we're not quite sure. Belief, in its simplest definition, is taking God at His word. It's saying that even though I don't see how, even though I don't understand why, even though I've never seen it happen before, even though I can't imagine when,… I'm choosing to believe.

Ordering from
Jesus' Soul Food Menu:

Step 1 -   Believe in Jesus
                 John 6:29

Step 2 -

Day 5
Come and Get It!

I can still feel the sudden hunger pains of my childhood that would strike me out of nowhere as I was riding my bike down the street, jumping on the trampoline, or playing at a friend's house. I didn't even have to wait for the dinner bell that my mom would ring through the neighborhood each evening to know it was time to eat. Come 6:00 I was hungry and ready for supper. And, because I'm blessed with a great mom who fulfilled her responsibilities to her family and is a super cook to boot, I knew I could count on her to feed me each night (and any other time as well).

So what would I do? Well, I can assure you I didn't just continue to ride my bike around, telling myself over and over that mom would feed me. And I didn't continue to jump on the trampoline while simply visualizing the feast spread out on our dining room table. I may have occasionally stayed at a friend's house to eat dinner only to find that her mom didn't make mashed potatoes the way my mom did and they didn't have sweet tea either. I knew if I wanted to eat I needed to head home, wash my hands, and sit down at my mom's table.

Pardon me if I've gotten your mouth salivating for a good home-cooked meal, but I think it's only appropriate that we're a little hungry as we approach this particular Bible study each day. Physical hunger and the rumbling of the tummy serve as stark reminders of the power and drive of our soul hungers. And today we're going to continue to learn exactly how we can get our soul hungers satisfied by the One who has promised us "food which endures to eternal life."

Please pause to pray, asking the Holy Spirit to direct your study and open your eyes to His teaching.

_____ I stopped to pray before proceeding with today's Bible study.

What is step one in ordering from Jesus' soul food menu? (Hint: We learned this step in our previous lesson and it's found in John 6:29.)

Hopefully you recalled that we first have to believe in Jesus in order to partake of the satisfying food He offers. As we studied earlier, believing in Him involves more than mental assent that He exists. More extensively, it requires that we be fully convinced that He is who He says He is and that He can and will do what He says He will do. Belief requires that we entrust ourselves and our desires to Him, counting on Him alone to meet those needs.

But there's more. I can believe that Jesus will satisfy my hungers, but unless I follow through with those beliefs I'll never get fed.

Please read John 6:29-33. Mark these verses as you have the previous ones, noting all references to *Jesus*, *the crowd*, *bread* or *food*, *God the Father*, and *work*. Also mark the word *believe*. Take your time!

While we won't spend a lot of time in these scriptures today, I want us to continue to follow along with Jesus' conversation with the hungry crowd. Allow me to ask you a few questions about this passage and then we'll move on. But feel free to note anything additional you learn that might shed light on our subject.

Was the crowd of hungry people ready to believe Jesus? Why do you answer as you do?

What did they want from Jesus before they would "*pisteuo*" or believe Him?

Who do they seem to believe gave the Israelites manna while they were in the wilderness?

List everything you find out in these verses about the "bread out of heaven."

Additional notes or summary of findings:

Now we get to our focal verses. I'm still not sure that at the conclusion of verse 33 the people are ready to believe in Jesus to the degree which He is asking. In fact, we'll learn later on that most of them did not trust Him that much. But they do seem to realize Jesus is offering them something pretty amazing and they want to learn all they can about how to obtain this bread. It reminds me of some of my shopping trips. I see something I like and want, but I'm not sure I want to pay the price on the tag. Still, I try it on, consider what other garments I could wear it with, and even ask the sales lady to put it on hold while I think about it. But often I never go back and buy the item. I inquired, but I did not receive the item of inquiry because I hadn't followed through.

Please read John 6:34-36, marking every reference to *Jesus, the crowd, bread* or *food, believes,* and time.

What is the crowd's response to Jesus' description of the "bread out of heaven" in verse 34?

How does Jesus identify Himself in John 6:35?

In verse 35 we find Step 2 for being fed by Jesus that which satisfies completely. Read the verse carefully and tell me what you think Step 2 is.

Step 2 - _____ _to_ _____

Earlier I shared my memories of how my mom faithfully supplied dinner for me and my family as I was growing up. I told you how I was very secure in my belief that my mother would have a good and ample meal waiting for me each evening when I returned home from my childhood adventures. I was a blessed child because I had a faithful, responsible, and loving mom who always met my needs for food. But it wasn't enough to know that my mom would and could faithfully feed me. I had to *go to her* to receive that satisfying meal. Sounds simple, I know. But could it be that this is the step that is causing some of us the most frustration in getting our soul hungers met?

In case you still are unconvinced that it's that big of a deal to "come to Jesus" in order to receive the bread of life He promises, let's look at a few other scriptures for confirmation.

Please read and summarize the following scriptures.

Matthew 11:28 –

Matthew 19:21 –

Mark 10:14-16 –

What common words were found in each passage or verse?

Now read Luke 14:15-27. In this passage Jesus first tells a story to His dinner partner that illustrates perfectly the importance of *coming* to Him. Then He goes on to share with the crowd the cost of *not coming* to Him.

No more time for my pontificating! I'm going to leave you on your own as we close today's lesson. Besides, you've studied the same scriptures I have. You can pull the juicy morsels out just as easily as I can. I pose one final question and urge you to think on it for a while. It's not a question meant to be applied to the "crowd." It's meant for you personally.

When you are hungry – and we all get hungry – *why* **don't you "come to Jesus?"**

Do you believe He faithfully has dinner waiting for you every day? Then come and get it!

Ordering from
Jesus' Soul Food Menu:

Step 1 -   Believe in Jesus
           John 6:29

Step 2 -   Come to Jesus
           John 6:35

Summary

This week we've learned that we all have soul hungers, unique and yet common among us. Fortunately, Jesus understands and acknowledges those hungers. He is not offended or taken by surprise when we long for companionship or acceptance. He does not brush us off when we hunger for a little appreciation or love. And He certainly isn't appalled by our desire for significance and worth. In fact, He created us to hunger after these things and others so that we would be drawn to Him, the source of all that truly satisfies our souls.

Because our hungers are often strong and compelling, they sometimes drive us to other sources besides Christ where we try in vain to get our fill. The result is frustration, unhealthy relationships, dangerous addictions, and crippling emotional problems. We've mistakenly believed that other people, experiences, and things could feed our souls and, because they can't and don't, we're belly-aching over our lack of fulfillment. Or perhaps we're starving in silence, believing ourselves to be some sort of martyrs. Actually, nothing could be further from the truth. We're just the King's kids who refuse to take their rightful seat at the table.

But we've also learned that Jesus has willingly and lovingly offered to satisfy our every hunger. He claims to be the bread of life, the food that endures and satisfies as nothing else can. How do we obtain this filling bread, this manna from heaven? We believe that He is all He says He is and then we willingly, eagerly, and expectantly come to Him to receive the hardy meal He has promised.

Sweet sister, this is no time to eat like a bird! Put on a big bib if you need to, prepare to get your hands a little messy, pull up a chair to the table, and put your napkin in your lap. Your Father has called you to dinner. Over the next several weeks we will continue to learn how we can get more than a little satisfaction from the feast He has provided.

Week 1
Discussion Questions

1. Are you surprised by Jesus' desire to feed the multitude (John 6:1-14) their evening meal? Why or why not?

2. Not only was Jesus' feeding of the 5,000 a practical and generous miracle that met a real need among the people; but it also served as a sort of visual lesson about how Jesus feeds us spiritually. Discuss any principles you see taught in this momentous lesson.

3. What are some of the soul hungers you see in teenagers today? What do you see these unfulfilled hungers driving them to?

4. The crowds' hunger drove them across a sea to seek out and follow Jesus. If you are comfortable with sharing, name some of the "places" your hungers have driven you to in the past. What were the results?

5. On day three, we learned that the people were willing to work for the fantastic food Jesus described to them. In what ways do we try to "work" for the food that satisfies our souls?

6. What is the first step for placing our order with Jesus, so to speak, for soul nourishing food? Exactly what does that first step entail? How is it different from just mental assent that Jesus exists?

7. How can you increase your belief in Jesus?

8. What is the difference between *believing* in Jesus and His ability to provide for your need and actually *coming* to Him for provision? Why might some Christians, even those who know their Bible and attend church faithfully, struggle with this concept?

Week 2 - Can't Get No Satisfaction?

We're going to do something a little unusual for a Bible study. While you would expect us to move forward this week, we're taking a step back.

It was important last week to go ahead and nail down the fact that Jesus is the one who can satisfy our souls. He alone can fulfill every soul desire. When we believe He is who He says He is and we go to Him to have every need met, He will and does satisfy like no other.

But the sad truth is that many of us do not go to Jesus with our hungers. Instead we go through our days like starving beggars holding out our tin cups, asking anyone and everyone to put in a little something. We long to be full of the good stuff, but we settle instead for cheap substitutes. And then, like a child who has filled up on sugary snacks, we are soon hungry again and looking for our next meal.

This week, before we discover exactly how to create a lifestyle of eating at the King's table, we will examine what happens when we don't. We're going to see what happens when we "can't get no satisfaction."

> One more thing. You'll remember last week I reminded you at the beginning of each lesson to spend some time in prayer, asking for the Holy Spirit to teach you. This week I'll leave that up to you.
>
> It's so important to ask God to open our eyes to His truths. The Bible teaches us that the natural woman can't understand the things of God; only the woman who has the Holy Spirit guiding her in all truth can learn from God. Be sure to invoke His presence and yield to His teaching each day.

Day 1
When I'm Not Happy...

Raise your hand if you've heard the saying, "If Mama ain't happy, ain't nobody happy!" One, two… three… four…. Ok, we've all heard it and lived it out I'm sure. Unfortunately this saying is all too true, not only in our households, but in schools, businesses, churches, you name it. If one key person is disgruntled and unhappy, their sour disposition rubs off on everyone else faster than the odor of garlic permeates your kitchen.

We've all laughed at this witty little maxim and even chuckled about how well it fits us, but honestly, do we want to have that kind of affect on those around us? Do we want to spread the odor of our discontent? In fact, let's examine that.

The Bible does speak of an aroma that is to permeate our lives and stimulate the senses of those around us. It's not the putrid odor of discontent, but the refreshing scent of one who knows Christ.

Please read 2 Corinthians 2:14-16 and Ephesians 5:1-2. Mark the words *fragrance* **and** *aroma* **in the same distinguishing way in both passages. After carefully reading the scriptures, complete the chart below with any information you can find to go in the appropriate columns. I'll get you started.**

The Aroma of Christ

Scripture Passage	Description of aroma/fragrance	How it is demonstrated
2 Corinthians 2:14-16	*sweet aroma*	*Manifested by God through us*
Ephesians 5:1-2		

Our attitudes and behavior affect those around us in either a positive or damaging way. And we don't just cause the people in our realm of influence to have either a bad day or a good one. More importantly, we draw them closer to God by spreading the sweet aroma of Christ or we drive them further from Him with the stench of our discontent. So our attitudes, words and behaviors are important to the building up or tearing down of God's kingdom.

We've established that our behavior can either set a tone for godliness and peace or create disharmony and mayhem. But how are our attitudes, words, and actions tied to our sense of soul satisfaction? Is my behavior really dependent upon my sense of fullness? Do I really spread the sweet aroma of Christ when I am full and satisfied from feasting on the Living Bread, but the odor of selfishness and discontent when I am lacking?

Please read James 4:1-3 in your Bible. Then answer the following questions based on this passage. We'll take it verse by verse.

1. What problem is the author, James, trying to get to the bottom of? (verse 1)

2. According to James, what is causing the inner battle within the individual believers he is addressing? (verse 1)

3. According to verse 2, what happens when a person wants something and doesn't get it?

4. In verse 2, James hints at a plausible solution to the believers' constant condition of discontent. What does he suggests would solve the problem?

5. In verse 3 James says believers sometimes ask God for what they want but they still go lacking. Why is that? (Tuck that answer away for a future lesson.)

According to James 4:1-3, when desires go unmet we *will* behave badly. First those unmet desires cause an inner turmoil that shows up in our attitudes, our tone of voice, and our countenance. We can go through all the right motions for a while, but that inner battle takes its toll – it robs us of our peace, takes our joy, saps our energy and steals the love we intended to share with others.

Next, the battle moves from the inside to the outside, where the toll is even more costly. We act out our frustrations and usually hurt anyone and anything within swinging distance, so to speak. The words James uses to describe the potential outcomes of our inner frustration are important.

Look over the following definitions for the words in James 4:1 & 2. Think about them carefully and jot down any significant implications that come to mind.

conflicts – disputes, outbursts, skirmishes

quarrels – long term wars; wars that last indefinitely with continuing results

commit murder – to become a murderer, one who kills; to kill; to put to death

Sweet sister, I battled for years with the inability to keep my emotions and my actions in check. I blamed my moodiness and my unpredictable behavior on raging hormones, lack of sleep, unreasonable people, difficult circumstances, you name it – anything to take the responsibility for my actions off my shoulders. I claimed my husband wasn't meeting my needs and wasn't paying me enough attention. I decided my children did not appreciate me enough. I grew resentful when friends didn't drop everything to meet my needs. I stayed frustrated with the lack of fulfillment I drew from my job as a fulltime homemaker. Bottom line: I had unfulfilled needs and it was everyone else's fault. I was miserable and I was making other people miserable, too.

In fact, I still have days when I owe apologies to other people for my flightiness. But I've come to terms with the fact that I am the only one to blame for my poor conduct. On those days that I am a little testy (that's what I prefer to call it, thank you) I can do a soul check and find nine times out of ten that I'm running on empty. My neediness is causing an inner battle that eventually sucks the life out of my world. That's when I lose my temper easily and say things I later regret. Then I begin building cases against other people one unforgiven offense on top of another. Finally, I begin to scheme about how I'm going to let them all have it. Conflicts lead to quarrels and those quarrels lead to murder.

Fortunately I've finally come to understand the truth of James 4:1-2. When I am quarrelsome and difficult it is usually because I have unmet needs. I've also learned to heed James' implied advice, to ask God to meet my needs instead of expecting other people somehow to fulfill those desires. It is largely out of this life-changing lesson that I was inspired to write such a study and share biblical principles with you. Dear friend, going to Jesus, the Bread of Life, to have my needs met has made a significant difference in my life. It can do the same for you, too.

Look over the following lists of emotions and behaviors. Put a check by any that you sometimes struggle with.

Emotions

_____self-pity

_____jealousy

_____depression

_____resentment

_____exhaustion

_____emptiness

_____bitterness

_____impatience

_____intolerance

_____selfishness

_____haughtiness

_____weariness

_____complacency

_____rage

_____unexplained sadness

_____isolation

Behaviors

_____raising my voice in anger

_____slamming doors

_____withdrawing

_____silent treatment

_____neglecting responsibilities

_____arguing

_____losing temper easily

_____frowning and scowling

_____being sarcastic or critical

_____not listening to others

_____being rude to others

_____being lazy

_____doing things half way/compromising

_____acting destructively/dangerously

_____blaming others for your unhappiness

_____refusing to apologize

Do you ever feel like you're trying to operate on empty? Like everyone needs something from you and you have nothing to give? The truth is we each *do* have something to offer the other people in our lives, but often we cling to what we could give others because we are not having our own needs met. And because God made us to live in relationship with one another, He expects us to help meet the needs of others. We'll talk about proper boundaries in those relationships later, but in healthy relationships we should be willing to give of ourselves. However, we are not likely to give when we are experiencing one or more of the emotions on the above list. Instead we are very prone to act according to one or more of the actions in the column on the right

.

Please read Philippians 2:3-4 in your Bible.

According to this passage, we are to: (put a check beside the correct answers)

_____ concentrate on getting our own needs met.

_____ operate out of selfishness.

_____ spend more time thinking about others than myself.

_____ look for ways to meet the needs of others.

Tall order... I can't possibly live that way if I am focused on my own unmet needs.

Picture yourself drinking your favorite iced coffee or soft drink at a quiet bookstore. You've been reading your magazine and sipping a sweet, refreshing beverage through a straw in quiet solitude. Suddenly you realize you've drained the cup dry. How do you know? You and everyone within earshot hear the loud, obnoxious slurping noise as you suck air and a few remaining drops through the straw. Swwwwwrrrp! Go ahead. Make that sound and note how obnoxious it is.

That, dear friend, is the same sound our lives make when we try to give to others out of our emptiness instead of our bounty. It's the soundtrack of our lives when we resent the happiness and contentment of everyone around us because our own cup is empty and we are desperately searching for one more drop. And it is the offensive noise our lives make when we try to send a covert message to others that says, "Hey! My cup is empty! Haven't you noticed? What are *you* going to do about it?"

But what about when my cup really is dry? What about those days when I have given and given until I have no more to give? What if I have no bounty to draw from? Let's see what the apostle Paul had to say.

Read Philippians 2:17-18 in your Bible. How do you think Paul would answer our questions?

If I am desperately looking for fulfillment in all the wrong places, I will surely begrudge having to pour out the little I have managed to accumulate. When I give of myself to others, it will be with resentment and even anger. Not only will I feel empty and cheated, but I will grow increasingly bitter every time someone needs something from me.

However, if I am going to Jesus to have my soul hungers met, then I can give away every last drop of that which is in me and count it all joy because I know where to go for a refill. So, go to the Living Water and drink with gusto. We'll talk more later about how to do that, but meanwhile just run to Him, the One who wants to fill you up with good things that last into eternity.

∿

Day 2
Fooling Ourselves with Empty Wells

Yesterday we looked at the feelings, attitudes, and general behaviors that result from running on empty. Because our demeanors, words and actions affect those around us, our famished souls can cause a stench that not only offends but ultimately drives away the very people we love. Our desperate attempts to hold onto every last drop of satisfaction we have managed to acquire will cause us to sound like greedy children slurping one more drop from an empty cup. We'll resent anyone who asks us to "share" from our cup and we'll grow bitter when it looks like others have more than we do. But alas, the damage continues.

When I first began to realize my feelings of emptiness were causing stress on my relationships, I panicked and tried to set things right. I didn't want to chase away my loved ones with my bad behavior and I certainly didn't want to be a whiny wife or an unhappy mother. I didn't want the important people in my life to be repulsed by my neediness.

Have you ever had similar feelings? Explain.

When I realized my neediness was causing me to behave badly, I decided to take care of the problem. First, I made a more concerted effort to have a daily quiet time and to study my Bible, but those things seemed like temporary fixes. I would feel full and satisfied as I sat at the kitchen table with my Bible, but shortly after leaving the table, depending on the events of the day, I could feel just as empty as the coffee cup I had drained during my quiet time. Going through the motions of very important and valid spiritual disciplines was not enough. Spiritual activity does not necessarily yield spiritual fullness.

Because I assumed I was doing all I could spiritually to satisfy my soul, I determined I needed to look in other directions for additional fulfillment. It wasn't that Jesus couldn't meet my every need; rather that I wasn't really allowing Him or even inviting Him to. We'll talk more later about how to truly eat from the Bread of Life so that He completely fills your cup. But for now let's explore what happens when we get up from His table and move on to other resources while still hungry.

Please read Leviticus 19:4. Write the first four words of this scripture below.

_____   _____   _____   _____

When we do not find complete satisfaction in the Lord, we tend to *turn away to* other sources for filling. God is not surprised by this abandonment. He so expects it that He warns us of our tendency to do that very thing. Like a child who unpacks a healthy and delicious lunch his mother has prepared for him but then notices his neighbor's lunch box full of cake and potato chips, we are prone to reach for that which *looks* more satisfying. And so we either turn to idols that are presented in pretty packages for the picking or we create ones to fit our own liking.

Read the following scriptures and summarize any pertinent information you find about idols.

Isaiah 44:9-20; Jeremiah 10:1-15; Jeremiah 17:5-8 (not all idols are stone or wood, many are flesh and blood); and Jonah 2:8.

What idols are:	Why we turn to them:	What happens when we do:

Hopefully you noticed that idols are those things which pull our allegiance and trust away from God. Just like in Leviticus 19:4, when we "turn to" idols we "turn from" God. We create or obtain idols because we believe they will somehow do something for us that God cannot or will not do. We spend time with them, put them in a place of prominence in our lives, trust that they will meet our needs, and protect them at all costs.

We turn to idols most often because we feel something is missing in our lives. Whether we crave more affirmation, additional safety and protection, more love and attention, or more excitement and joy, we turn to idols for that which we feel we are lacking.

Often we turn to idols because we are confused. Isaiah 44:18-20 infers that as we turn away from God and veer away from His light and illumination we become clouded in our thinking, as well as deceived. According to Isaiah, our deceived heart has the power to turn us toward an idol that we would otherwise never dream of going to for fulfillment. That is why we must carefully protect our hearts and minds by sticking close to the source of all true fulfillment. When we are shaky in our relationship with Jesus, our searching hearts often lead us to idols that seemingly promise to meet all our heart's desires.

But without fail the idol is a deception. As Isaiah 44:10-11 says, the idol does not profit us and ultimately puts us to shame. Perhaps you've been there. I have. I've walked away from idols only to look back and hang my head in shame, amazed that I could have been so gullible, so easily duped. For a while the idol seemed good, wholesome, right, harmless, and satisfying. But then, as I stepped back into the illumination of God's Word, I saw the idol for what it was and I was ashamed of all the time and energy I had invested, all the times I had defended my allegiance to it, and/or all the admiration I had devoted it. This has happened more than once in my life, I'm sad to say. But I am also thankful that God never leaves me soaking in my shame. He restores me and renews my joy if I confess my waywardness, forsake my idol, and return to Him.

So we don't fall into the common trap of assuming all idols are stone statues or wooden carvings, let's explore some idols that woo the modern woman.

Put an X beside every idol listed that either you have been drawn to or you know of someone who has. In other words, indicate the idols with which you are familiar. You'll notice many of these things are not bad in or of themselves. But when an attachment or devotion to them draws someone away from God, they become an idol. Also, if someone places unhealthy and unrealistic expectations on these things or people, they become idols.

_____ wardrobe, clothing	_____ a man, boyfriend, husband
_____ wealth	_____ success, affirmation, awards
_____ house, home, decorating	_____ exercise, fitness, losing weight
_____ food	_____ appearance, beauty
_____ girlfriend, relationship	_____ your child
_____ drugs, alcohol, prescription drugs	_____ work, accomplishment
_____ reading, escape, fantasy	_____ television shows, soap operas
_____ sleep	_____ travel, pleasure, spas
_____ video games	_____ Internet, Facebook, chat rooms
_____ pornography, sexual websites	_____ sex
_____ ministry, service, church	_____ gambling, gaming
_____ a celebrity, star, performer	_____ cigarettes
_____ chocolate	_____ gossip, entertainment news
_____ perfectionism	_____ spending money, shopping
_____ coffee, caffeine, colas	

I realize I've asked for a certain degree of vulnerability. I asked you to indicate forms of idolatry you are familiar with either on a first or second-hand basis so you could mark them with some sense of safety, not worrying that someone would see your list and judge you. However, it is still not easy to be real about such things.

Some of your experience may not be in the past, but in the present. You or I can stumble upon and become drawn in by an idol at the most unexpected time. Whenever our guard is down and we are vulnerable due to some unmet needs, we are very prone to develop an idolatrous relationship with a person, a thing, or an experience. As I mentioned earlier, I've been there more than once.

If you are struggling with an idol today, you have my compassion. Dear friend, please do not let the enemy convince you that you have fallen into some sort of obsession that is unique to you. If he persuades you that your situation is unique, that you are a hopeless case, that you are the only one who understands, then he will tighten his grip on you and further your captivity.

Before we go any further today, let's honestly and prayerfully lay our hearts before God, asking Him to identify for us any idolatry that has seeped into our lives.

Please mark the following True and False statements, making any pertinent notes along the way that might help you better assess your attachment to idols, if there is any.

T or F?

_____ There is something that consumes much of my thought life. My thoughts seem to revolve around this thing, activity or person more than they should.

_____ When I consider my spending habits, I realize I spend an inordinate amount of money on a certain thing, activity or person.

_____ I find myself often defending the amount of time or money I spend on a certain person, thing or activity.

_____ I go out of my way, changing plans and manipulating circumstances, in order to spend more time on a certain thing, activity or person.

_____ Friends and/or family members have questioned me about my allegiance to, obsession with or devotion to a certain thing, activity or person.

_____ I have questioned my own absorption with a certain thing, activity or person.

_____ I am not as interested in Bible study, church involvement, prayer, and/or worship time as I have been in the past.

_____ I feel like something is standing between me and God. I don't feel as close to Him as I have in the past.

_____ I find myself using a particular thing, activity or person to help me cope with life stresses and issues. It is almost as though I want to "run to" that thing, activity or person when trouble strikes.

_____ I talk about a certain thing, activity or person a lot, maybe even too much.

_____ I have recently felt guilty about my devotion to or need of a certain thing, activity or person.

_____ I find that a particular thing, activity or person gives me a sense of relief, contentment, or joy that I can't seem to get anywhere else, even if it is short-lived.

The True/False exercise either pricked your conscience or it didn't. There was no need to over-analyze the statements. If you have formed an idolatrous relationship with anything or anyone, it should have surfaced easily enough as you went through the exercise. If you marked one or more of the statements as true, you might spend some time reflecting on your answer(s). My guess is that if you have an idol, you already know it anyway. When I have formed an idol and worshipped that idol, I have known it. The problem wasn't identifying it, but being honest about it and walking away.

Still, I felt it was important to provide us with some fairly trustworthy measuring sticks that we can use to measure our affections and devotions. The statements I used in this exercise can also help us steer clear of idols in the future.

Finally, let's read one more important passage from the Bible as we wrap up today's lesson.

Please read Jeremiah 2:1-13. Answer the following questions based on what you read.

1. What does the Lord remember about His people? (2:2)

2. What does God accuse His children of doing in verse 5?

3. What important question did the people and the priests neglect to ask, according to verses 6 and 8?

4. What kinds of things did the prophets and the people follow after, according to verses 8 and 11?

5. What is heaven's reaction to the people's behavior, according to verse 12?

6. What two evils have God's people committed, according to verse 13?

7. How does God describe Himself in verse 13?

8. How does He describe the places the people have gone in order to get their needs met? (v. 13)

A cistern is a type of well or pit that is meant to hold water. In Jeremiah's day such a well would potentially offer much needed and anticipated refreshment for the one who put his bucket down into the hewn hole to draw water. But the cisterns described in Jeremiah 2:13 are broken, cracked, and can hold no water. They are faulty and do not deliver the anticipated refreshment.

God is accusing His people of forsaking Him, the dependable fountain of living waters, and creating for themselves cisterns from which they plan to get what they need instead of going to Him. They have *turned from Him* (remember our definition of idols) and gone instead to a source of fulfillment of their own making. And they've paid the price. Isn't it interesting that God describes Himself as a fountain, a water source that automatically bubbles up water past the surface for easy drinking? On the other hand, the people have dug cisterns where the water, if there had been any, would be much more difficult to acquire.

Dear friend, when we either don't know the God who satisfies or we don't understand how to reach out and draw our nourishment from His overflowing fountain, we tend to dig cisterns for ourselves as well, thinking we can somehow get our soul needs met. But those cisterns inevitably crack and any fulfillment they once offered slowly leaks out the bottom, leaving them dry and leaving us with empty buckets.

Let the circles below signify the broken, dry cisterns we sometimes visit in an effort to have our soul thirsts quenched. Write the names of cisterns you have dug, either recently or in the past, on the circles. For instance, you might label one "food" or "career" or "children" or "smoking."

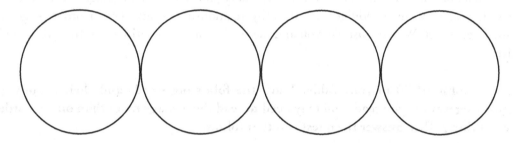

Now, choose today to walk away from those broken cisterns and instead cry out to God, the fountain of living waters. Put an X on each cistern as you confess your idol to God and commit to drinking from His abundant fountain instead.

Sweet sister, the way I see it, today's lesson is really the crux of this Bible study. As I've already mentioned, the reason I felt compelled to write this study is because I had lived from a state of emptiness, even as a believer, for years. I knew God, but continued to dig my own cisterns in my effort to find satisfaction in life. I would try one worthless, profitless idol after another, sometimes finding just enough temporary satisfaction to keep me coming back for more. Then, once I realized the cistern was cracked or the idol was nothing more than a scarecrow in a corn patch, I'd try to abandon it. But often by then an attachment or even addiction had been formed. And, in some cases, damage had been done to my reputation, my conscience, and my integrity. In order to escape the bondage I had allowed myself to fall into, I had my work cut out for me. Each time God extended His grace and His power to me, providing all I needed to turn away from the substitute and back to the Real Thing. He will do the same for you if you find yourself in that difficult place today.

But the greater work was done in my life when I began to understand the destructive pattern I had fallen into. I realized it wasn't enough to simply stay away from idols. I didn't just lay my shovel down and quit digging cisterns. Instead, I learned to drink fully from the fountain of living waters.

I learned to eat my fill from the Bread of Life. I learned that there is one who can satisfy me so completely that I never have to look to any other source for fulfillment again.

∞

Day 3

Sticky Relationships

As I watched the young mom apply the finishing touches to her tiny daughter's makeup, I cringed with empathy. She would later watch her four-year-old daughter saunter down the runway, modeling her shimmery pink pageant dress with a masterful pirouette. The judges deemed this young child's performance worthy of a huge trophy, which she would add to the others she'd collected. But the mother was the one with joyful tears in her eyes and a lump in her throat, while the little girl seemed oblivious to the significance of her accomplishment.

Watching this segment on an evening news show reminded me there are countless varieties of unhealthy relationships. While many women will never forsake their marriage for another man, countless Christian women indulge in unhealthy relationships every day in order to get their unsatisfied needs met. Women just like you and me search for a little satisfaction from the people in their lives.

Please read John 4:1-30 in your Bible. Mark the following words and their synonyms in distinguishing ways as you read. You may need to read the passage more than once in order to catch everything. Then answer the questions that follow.

- drink
- thirst
- water (mark "living water" a little differently, giving it extra significance)
- husband

1. Though Jesus began the conversation with the Samaritan woman by asking *her* for a drink of water, what does *He* eventually offer her? (vs. 10)

2. What claims does Jesus make about this special water?

3. What is the woman's initial reaction when she hears what this special water will provide?

4. Once the woman decides she wants the water Jesus offers, what does Jesus request of her?

5. Describe the woman's marital state with as much detail as you can.

6. Why do you think Jesus brought up her relationship with men at this point?

7. What significant thing begins to happen in the woman's mind once Jesus accurately describes her marital state to her? (vs. 19)

8. Do you think it might be significant that the woman left her water jar behind when she ran off to the city to tell everyone else about her encounter with Jesus? (vs. 28) Why or why not?

It's just another ordinary day for this woman of Samaria. She has journeyed to the well outside of town late in the evening, probably in an effort to avoid the scornful stares of the other women from town who would have been at the well earlier in the day. Having had five husbands and now living with a man to whom she is not married, this woman undoubtedly had few good girlfriends with whom to do her daily chores.

Isn't it interesting that Jesus, knowing the hearts of all people, began talking with this woman about water, about thirst? Jesus knew this woman was thirsty for something more than well water. She had an unquenchable thirst that had driven her to one unhealthy relationship after another.

And so Jesus offered this woman something that could truly satisfy her—living water. But before He would tell her how she could acquire this living water, water that would leave her completely satisfied and even overflow in her, he would require she be honest about where she had been searching for satisfaction up to this point in her life. He knew she had been going from man to man in an attempt to have her soul needs met, but he wanted *her* to realize what she had been doing as well. She would need to acknowledge that indeed she was thirsty and had been going to men to have that thirst quenched. In Jesus' simple summation of her marital state He managed to pierce her heart and drive home the fact that her constant thirst was *driving* her life. We know she got His message loud and clear because at this point she recognizes that He has a special ability to see deep inside of her, to know her thoughts and desires. Thus, she calls Him a prophet.

Sister, it is time for us to be honest about where we are going for our satisfaction.

Women are especially designed for close and intimate relationships. We thrive on them. More so than men, we care about our relationships, tend to them, fret over them, and value them. Consider this. When men introduce themselves to each other they often begin the process of getting to know one another by saying something like, "So what do you do for a living?" Women, on the other hand, more often than not begin with, "Are you married? Do you have children?" As women we actually tend to define ourselves by our relationships.

Relationships are a good thing. God created us for relationship. He saw that man was alone in the garden and decided that wasn't good. Man needed a relationship, so God created woman, a relationship expert. God tells us in His Word over and over how to live in relationship with other people. He wants us to have harmonious, deep and mutually edifying relationships. Jesus lived in relationship with His earthly family and walked for three years in the constant companionship of twelve good friends and countless others. Relationships in and of themselves are not bad. They are, in fact, very good.

But unhealthy relationships are not good.

How would you define an unhealthy relationship?

Most of us are familiar with the term codependency, though few of us understand it by definition. According to Jean M. LaCour, Ph.D., author of *Counseling the Codependent: A Christian Perspective Utilizing Temperament*, "In the broadest sense, codependency can be defined as an addiction to people, behaviors, or things. Codependency is the fallacy of trying to control interior feelings by controlling people, things, and events on the outside."[1] For the purpose of today's lesson, we want simply to focus on codependent relationships between people.

How do you know if you are in a codependent relationship? LaCour says in a codependent relationship one person actually becomes addicted to another.

> In this interpersonal codependency, the person has become so extensively involved in the other person that the sense of self—personal identity—is severely restricted, crowded out by that other person's identity and problems. There are severe personal boundary problems in knowing where "I end and you begin." [2]

Remember when we talked about idols and broken cisterns in yesterday's lesson? When a person or a relationship with a particular person becomes an idol, that relationship becomes a codependent one. When you consistently go to a particular person to have your needs met like you would go to a well or cistern for water, that relationship becomes codependent.

I'm not a psychiatrist, nor do I play one on television, so I don't want to wade into waters that are clearly over my head. But even here in the shallow end of this subject you and I can learn a few indicators of unhealthy, codependent relationships so we can honestly evaluate the relationships we are currently in and better navigate future ones.

---

1   Jean M. LaCour, Ph.D., *Counseling the Codependent: A Christian Perspective Utilizing Temperament*, 2nd ed. (Jean M. LaCour and The National Christian Counselors Association, 1996), p. 4

2   Jean LaCour, Ph.D., *Counseling the Codependent: A Christian Perspective Utilizing Temperament*, 2nd ed., p. 4

I'm providing you with a number of factors that indicate unhealthiness in a relationship. I've provided space for you to put a check beside those that describe a current or past relationship. However, if you'd rather not mark them, I certainly understand. Remember, I've been in situations where I could possibly mark most of these indicators, but I probably wouldn't for the sake of privacy. But I encourage you to spend time honestly evaluating your relationships by these statements. What relationships? Your relationships with your husband, children, girlfriend, mother, sister, co-worker, pastor, you name it. Specifically, though, target any relationship you fear may be a little unhealthy.

For the sake of making this exercise really work for you, please name the specific relationship you will be evaluating. Naming the relationship here does not indicate it is unhealthy; it just gives you a specific relationship to focus on as you read the statements. Feel free to evaluate more than one.
I am evaluating my relationship with: _____

_____ I frequently feel jealous or possessive in this relationship.

_____ I desire exclusivity in this relationship and see other people as threats to the relationship.

_____ I'd rather spend time alone with this individual and I become frustrated when this doesn't happen or when other people intrude.

_____ I become angry or depressed when the other person withdraws even slightly.

_____ I have lost interest in other relationships and prefer this one.

_____ I have had sexual or romantic feelings or fantasies about this person.

_____ I spend a lot of time focusing on this person's problems, interests, or plans.

_____ I prefer not to make plans without consulting or involving this other person.

_____ I think about this person almost constantly.

_____ I get very disappointed when I realize this person has not considered my needs in any given situation. I expect this person to consider me at all times.

_____ I do not easily see this person's faults.

_____ I have made other people uneasy with my familiar and intimate treatment of this person.

_____ I talk about this person often.

_____ I even "speak for" this person at times.

_____ I am physically affectionate with this person beyond what is generally considered appropriate for this type of relationship.

_____ I've been defensive about this relationship when others have asked or commented about it.

_____ I dislike being away from this person for any length of time.

_____ I have secrets with this person.

_____ My conversations with this person often revolve around our feelings for each other.*

*This list is based loosely on a list provided by Lori Thorkelson Rentzel in *Emotional Dependency*.[3]

---

3 Lori Thorkelson Rentzel, *Emotional Dependency: A Threat to Close Friendships* (San Rafael, California: Exodus International).

If you found that a few or more of these statements described one of your current relationships, I compassionately suggest you take a long, hard look at the relationship. It's definitely not easy to take a step back from a relationship you have become so enmeshed in, but it may be necessary. Perhaps you could look over the list with another Christian who cares about you and who would be able to help you honestly evaluate your relationship. I realize that's a big step, but I have found there is great benefit in conducting all of my relationships out in the open. In the fresh air of accountability and transparency, my relationships can grow into what they are meant to be—opportunities for godly encouragement and joyful, sweet companionship.

Jesus wanted to give the Samaritan woman living water that would satisfy her soul thirsts and spring up like a bountiful well inside of her. But first He wanted her to see that she had been mistakenly going to men to have her soul needs met. If her choice was to keep going to another relationship for what only Jesus could offer, then she couldn't drink from His living water too. We can only drink from one fountain at a time.

If I am trying to quench my soul thirsts through an unhealthy attachment to my daughter, that well will eventually run dry and she will undoubtedly resent my neediness. If I insist that my husband meet my every need and jealously guard my marriage against even healthy interaction with others, my clinginess will eventually push him farther away and perhaps into the arms of someone less possessive. If I attach myself to another woman with the crazy glue of intimacy and emotion, we will head down a dangerous path that eventually ends in destruction. And if I continue to try to please my mother at all costs, craving her approval above all else, I will find that cistern is empty, too, and I will never have enough resources within me to give a healthy love to my own children.

Sweet friend, if you've been running to any of these or any other empty cistern for water, put your water jar down right where you are and run to Jesus instead. He alone will give you living water that satisfies your soul.

⟶⟋⟝⟋⟝⟋⟝⟋⟝⟋

Day 4
So We Cope

Yesterday we took a plunge into the concept of codependency, though I acknowledged that I could quickly get in over my head if I wasn't cautious. Today we'll continue to wade in the shallow end of this subject as we look at how addictions can become fast but lousy substitutes for the satisfaction only Jesus can truly supply. I confess that I'm relying heavily on other people's knowledge at this point, but, unfortunately, I'm full of personal experience as well.

According to the Merriam-Webster Online Dictionary, to be an addict is "to devote or surrender (oneself) to something habitually or obsessively."

How does that definition compare to our definition of *idolatry*?

While the word addiction is not mentioned in the Bible, the problem of being surrendered to a substance or activity (or person, as we discussed yesterday) certainly exists in the Bible.

Read the following scriptures in your Bible and record any words used to describe the addict and how her addictions affect her.

Deuteronomy 21:18-20
Proverbs 20:1
Proverbs 23:20-21
Proverbs 23:29-35
Isaiah 5:11-12
Ephesians 5:18 (If your Bible uses the word *dissipation* and you don't know the meaning, look it up.)

Biblical description of an addict:

Biblical counselors agree that the root of addiction is not found in the addict's family background, her environment, or her biochemical make-up. While these factors may answer some questions concerning the addict's dysfunction and are often worth exploring, the key to understanding an individual's addictive behavior is found in Isaiah 5:11-12.

Reread Isaiah 5:11-12. What does the addict do, or more precisely *not do*, that causes him to be drawn over and over to the object of his obsession?

We were created with an inner desire and drive to worship something. We'll either worship the living God or we'll find something or someone else to give that honor to. If we're not even paying attention to the deeds of the Lord or considering what He is up to, both in our lives and in the world around us, we are certainly not worshiping Him. And if we're not worshiping God, truly acknowledging and honoring His character and His work, then we are probably worshiping something else on a consistent basis. That thing or person thus becomes the object of our addiction. It is an idol because not only does it persistently draw our attention and devotion, but it draws it away from the God who truly deserves it.

Once again we see that our idolatry, and the resulting addictive behavior, is rooted in a misdirected pursuit for fulfillment. If we go to Jesus, the Bread of Life and the Living Water, for that which we are lacking, we are not tempted to search for fulfillment through the dangerous and addictive substances and experiences that promise so much but offer so little.

Another term for an addiction is *learned behavior*. Learned behaviors are coping mechanisms that produce some degree of satisfactory results for the codependent. When a woman feels she needs something, whether it is a godly desire or an unhealthy and unholy one, she may learn to go to a certain substance or engage in a specific behavior in order to get what she wants. These results are often less than ideal and certainly don't last for long. More importantly, the satisfactory results are always coupled with dangerous and even deadly consequences. Finally, any behavior or substance that becomes a crutch for survival and a necessity for satisfaction eventually enslaves the person.

Examples of learned behaviors include:

- yelling
- smoking
- spending money excessively
- becoming silent and withdrawn
- over-eating
- drinking alcohol
- viewing pornography

This list is by no means exhaustive, as I'm sure you know. You'll also notice that some of these behaviors are not necessarily bad. For instance, it's fine to eat and spend money. It's also acceptable to surf the Internet, go shopping, or exercise. But when a woman tries to get her needs met over and over through a substance or behavior, whether it is intrinsically good and natural or harmful and sinful, the method of finding satisfaction becomes a learned behavior that helps her cope instead of thrive. Besides the fact that some substances (e.g., drugs, alcohol, cigarettes, chocolate) and behaviors (e.g., viewing pornography, exercising) are chemically addictive, many others (e.g., shopping, withdrawing, yelling) are addictive in nature simply because they produce results somewhat consistently.

Enough psychological babble! Let's get practical with this thing.

Read the following scenarios about women just like you and me. Then answer three questions which will help us understand better why we fall into addictive behaviors.

1. Lori is 33 years old and single. She's always wanted to marry, but Mr. Right hasn't come along. Lori longs for the companionship of a man and believes marriage indeed would solve so many of her problems. But Lori has decided marriage simply isn't in the cards for her. So she invests most of her time and energy in her work. Lori works long hours during the week and goes to the office most weekends. Though none of her colleagues ever take work home, she lugs her laptop home every evening so she can "get ahead." She hasn't been to church in months because she's just too exhausted to engage in the activities there.

- What do you think Lori's soul hungers for?

- How has she learned to cope with her unsatisfied hungers?

- What possible addiction has Lori developed because she is "coping" instead of going to Jesus for fulfillment?

2. Julie is an exhausted mother and school teacher. She loves her husband, her two children, and her job, but something is missing. Julie feels like she works and works at home and at school, but no one notices. Her parents always applauded her every move when she was growing up, but now no one seems to appreciate her for what she does for them. No one praises her efforts or notices her achievements. And so Julie eats. Stopping by the ice cream shop on the way home from work is like a little reward for her hard efforts. At dinner Julie helps herself to bountiful portions because "she deserves it." And before she goes to bed she usually treats herself to a little indulgence from her private stash of candies. Julie acknowledges she needs to lose some weight, but she just can't seem to break her attachment to good food.

- What do you think Julie's soul hungers for?

- How has she learned to cope with her unsatisfied hungers?

- What possible addiction has Julie developed because she is "coping" instead of going to Jesus for fulfillment?

3. Barbara is divorced and 55 years old. Her grown children live in other states and she rarely sees them. Barbara works as a dental hygienist and part-time at a local department store. To tell you the truth, Barbara is still brokenhearted over her divorce which was instigated by her husband five years ago. She always believed being a wife and mother was her primary purpose in life and now she is neither. Now, Barbara gains her greatest joy from buying things on EBay. She enjoys the whole system of bidding for items and shopping for the best buy. But she doesn't scour for bargains to save money; in fact, she spends most of her take-home pay on items like ceramic birds, table linens she never uses, garden statuettes, and large sets of antique china. She accumulates so much stuff she has to have garage sales to get rid of it all. Then she builds up her collections again.

- What do you think Barbara's soul hungers for?

- How has she learned to cope with her unsatisfied hungers?

- What possible addictions has Barbara developed because she is "coping" instead of going to Jesus for fulfillment?

It's easy enough to pinpoint someone else's coping mechanisms, to name someone else's addiction. But we often turn a blind eye to our own codependent behavior. Not only that, but we tend to sugarcoat our idolatrous habits. Rather than call them sins, we call them *vices* and we claim "we all deserve at least one, darling." Maybe it's time we get honest about our idolatry. Only then will we find our way back to the One who can truly satisfy.

Please turn in your Bible to Romans 6. I would love it if you would read the whole chapter, but if you're short for time, simply read the passages below and write down any facts or insights relevant to our study of addictions and codependency. (Hint: look for words like slave, master, obey, result, outcome, benefit.)

Romans 6:6-7 –

Romans 6:11-13 –

Romans 6:14 –

Romans 6:16 –

Romans 6:21-23 –

I trust that you carefully observed the scriptures from Romans and the Holy Spirit showed you some meaningful truths about addictions along with their powerful and enslaving nature. I also hope your saw that we are not meant to be slaves to anything but Christ and His righteousness.

I just want to point out one little thing I noticed as I looked back over the passage. If you're like me, you're looking for the practical application in this study. You may be saying, "Ok, I have some habits and some things I do often that bring about results. But how do I know if something is a good habit – like exercising for fitness and health – or if it's an addiction, a coping mechanism?"

Reread Romans 6:21 in your Bible. According to this scripture, what emotion *often* (not necessarily always) accompanies or follows that which enslaves us, the use of substances or behaviors to which we are addicted?

_____ Freedom _____ Joy _____ Shame _____ Boredom

Dear friend, God means for us to live abundantly full lives. He means for us to have joy and contentment and purpose and peace and freedom and victory. He means for us to experience all that is holy and good. But He wants to be the provider. In fact, only He *can* provide all that in a consistent

42

manner that is healthy and good for us. When a believer tries to create those things in her life through learned behaviors, shame will often whisper a convicting reminder that she is going to the wrong well for living water—an empty cistern, in fact. While God does not desire for us to *live* with shame, He does allow it to awaken us to our sin. Are you ignoring a wake-up call?

✧

Day 5
The Slippery Slope

Today I'd like to tell you a story. You can put your pen down and you won't need your Bible quite yet. Just pour something nice to drink, sit back, and meet Sarah.

Sarah could be your next door neighbor or your co-worker or your jogging buddy. She's someone with which you could easily be friends. She doesn't have anything especially peculiar in her background. Like most everyone else, she has a few quirky family members and friends. A few of them have said things or behaved in ways that have adversely affected her, but there's no one incident that even she would claim has scarred her for life.

Life has had its usual share of ups and downs for Sarah. She went through some difficult breakups with boyfriends in college, had a hard time landing a good job when she got out of school, found herself in a job where her boss skipped town without paying her, and watched all of her girlfriends marry before she even got engaged.

But life has also been good to Sarah. She's been blessed with generous parents and good friends. She did well in school and her accomplishments were celebrated and recognized by others. Finally she did get married and later had two healthy children. She was able to stay home with them even though she and her husband had to budget every penny.

Sarah is a Christian and has honestly tried to walk with the Lord ever since she asked Him into her heart at the age of eight. She has been active in her local church, consistently participated in Bible studies, had a daily quiet time with some degree of success, and attended huge women's events featuring the likes of Beth Moore, Kay Arthur, and Nancy Leigh DeMoss.

Still, as sweet and normal as Sarah's life has been, she will tell you that she has been enslaved to more than one addiction.

At one point Sarah used food to cope with loneliness and insecurity. Not only did she devour whole pizzas by herself, but she feasted with her eyes on the food section of women's magazines. Sarah visited grocery stores for the fun of it and watched cooking shows incessantly. In an attempt to not gain weight, she began to use laxatives as well as induce vomiting (bulimia). It was a costly and even deadly coping device, but it gave a sense of control to one who was very out of control. Eventually, Sarah recognized her unhealthy behavior for what it was. It scared her to death and she was able, by the grace of God, to stop binging and purging.

But the emptiness that had led Sarah to eat and purge had not been filled. She thought it had because she started running and the exercise took care of her weight gain. But the running just became her next addiction. She ran so much and so often that she lost weight quickly. In fact, her family and friends began asking her if she was losing too much weight. Sarah experienced a tinge of guilt each time someone asked probing questions, but her pride prevented her from listening to either the shame or the concerned voices.

Eventually Sarah stopped running as much and started eating a little better. She finally felt full and whole, but only because an old boyfriend re-entered her life. She began to believe that he was "the one," that he would complete her and they would face the world together. Finally, Sarah was in a relationship with a "godly" man, something she had always desired, and she felt completely happy.

Fortunately, when the godly boyfriend cheated on her, Sarah happened to be in a good place spiritually. So, even though she had been wounded, she felt like she was finally normal and healthy. Sensing that her emotional health was directly related to her spiritual discipline, she became even more involved in church and ministry than she had been before. She took courses on how to study the Bible and began teaching Bible studies. Sarah absolutely loved studying and teaching the Bible, but noticed that while others talked about falling more and more in love with Jesus, she just fell more and more in love with studying the Bible. It didn't feed her soul as much as it fed her intellect. Still, it was something to pacify the longings.

She soon became bored with studying the Bible. After all, it wasn't really meeting any emotional needs. She needed friends for that, Sarah reasoned. By this point in her life, she had moved far away from her family and friends because of her husband's job. She was a weary young mother and didn't really have many friends her age where she lived. For a while the cast of characters on the television show *Thirty-Something* became her pals. She insisted that her two preschoolers take their nap at one o'clock each afternoon to ensure that she get her fill from Hope and Michael and the gang. If her two children didn't cooperate with nap time, Sarah felt cheated and angry. When she was able to watch her show, she became so enmeshed in the characters' lives that she "worried" about them all evening. She finally realized she needed to stop watching *Thirty-Something* after she literally mourned Gary's death (Gary was one of the characters, not an actor).

Sarah continued to go through a series of obsessions ranging from reading romance novels incessantly, to surfing the internet for hours, to eating again. She attached herself to friends, insisting they give her more attention than reasonable. She even complained when her husband was just a few minutes late getting home from work, demanding that he spend more and more time with her.

Until one day, I don't really know exactly when, Sarah realized that she was miserable because nothing, *nothing* seemed to satisfy her. Instead of turning to another substance, person or activity, Sarah decided, on this particular day, to complain to Jesus about her lack of fulfillment. And you know what happened? Unlike her friends and her husband, Jesus didn't express His displeasure with her neediness. He didn't seem threatened by it or scared away by it. He didn't withdraw like some friends had done, and He didn't get frustrated like her well-intentioned husband had. In fact, instead of being put out with Sarah's neediness, He seemed to welcome it.

Drawn to the story of the woman at the well, Sarah considered for the first time all the different places she had been going to have her needs met. At a woman's conference that spring, she heard Nancy Leigh DeMoss launch an entire message from John 4. Sarah saw herself as the needy, misdirected, and confused woman to whom Jesus spoke so compassionately. And she wondered if He still offered living water to women who had dug one cracked cistern after another. She determined to try Him and see.

Sarah began to spill her emotions to Jesus on a regular basis. She would tell Him daily how she was feeling and what she felt like she needed. She would search His Word, not for academic lessons she could then teach to others, but for sustenance that would minister to her empty places. She would find truths about Jesus and how He alone could meet her needs. Then she'd remind Him of those promises, holding Him to His word. Finally, she would wait for Him to do His thing. She resisted the temptations (and they were there) to run to someone or something else with her empty water jar. She laid it at Jesus' feet instead and waited patiently for Him to fill it.

She noticed that often Jesus filled her empty places *through* a friend, her husband, or even her children. He sometimes met those needs through an affirming comment, a sweet smile, an interesting experience, a visit with her parents or even a particularly delicious meal. But Sarah learned to distinguish between the gift and the Giver, so she refrained from becoming attached to any one channel of God's blessings.

Finally, not only did Sarah feel much happier and more content, but she believed she had something to offer to others. When her children needed her, Sarah didn't resent the time and energy they required, but she gave of herself willingly and wholeheartedly. When her husband needed her, she didn't automatically check an internal scorecard where she tallied how much he'd done for her against how much she had done for him. She didn't need to keep score anymore. Jesus was supplying amply for her needs and she could afford to give from the overflow without expecting anything in return. And when she saw a need at church or in the community, she could joyfully contribute something, whereas before she feared she had nothing of any value to offer. In fact, she now had more of Jesus than she could possibly keep to herself. It appeared there was a fountain of water springing up within her and splashing all over the people in her life.

That's a true story, but it's not Sarah's story, as you may have guessed. It's mine. Even today when I no longer run from broken cistern to broken cistern with my empty water jar, I still have a hard time telling the story in first person, claiming it as my own. Everything I said in the story really happened, but not everything that really happened is in the story. Just like you would, I left out some very personal and painful trips I made to empty wells. I simply wanted to share enough of my story so you would know that I have been there, I've applied the principles we're learning in this study, and I've found them to work. They work because He is who He says He is.

Please turn in your Bible to Romans chapter 1. Please look for and mark the following words as you read verses 18 through 32:
- **God, Creator**
- **evident, clearly seen, understood (any synonyms)**
- **creature, creation**
- **exchanged**
- **"God gave them over"**
- **honor, give thanks, worship, served, acknowledge (these are all different expressions, but similar enough in this passage to mark them in the same way)**
- **filled, full**

I apologize for having you read so much, but we're about to get busy with more activity.

During our final day of looking at what happens when we don't get the satisfaction we naturally crave, I feel we need a firm understanding of the severity of the situation. I don't want us to end this week with the idea that handling our neediness is just an *option*. I haven't pointed out some of the common addictions that women fall into just so we can feel like we're in good company and carry on with our lives. Ladies, we have to fix this thing—this perpetual pursuit for soul satisfaction that takes us down slippery slope after slippery slope. Take it from one who's coped with life through a series of learned behaviors. It's not healthy, it's not abundant, and it's plain out dangerous. There's much to lose and nothing to gain from denial.

As you read in my story, I went through a lot of addictions—many I didn't and won't tell you about—without ever getting to the source of my problem. Perhaps you have also bounced from food issues to substance abuse to codependent relationships to workaholism to perfectionism to anger issues, or some other similar combination of coping devices. Please understand that just because you successfully exited one of those unhealthy behaviors doesn't mean you have found the fulfillment that will keep you from another. Only Jesus can meet your soul needs in a way that is healthy and holy. Only when you leave your water jar with Him will you find rest and quit running from one empty cistern to another.

Romans 1:18-32 offers a biblical explanation of what happens when we don't let God be God in our lives and make other things, people, or experiences the object of our affections instead. This passage refers to people who have felt the subtle nudges of shame we talked about yesterday. It has been brought to their attention that they are seeking fulfillment and satisfaction from an idol rather than the true God. They are making daily trips to empty, broken cisterns, but instead of acknowledging the problem, they continue the unhealthy pattern. Maybe they think it's innocent fun, a harmless diversion, or the only coping device for the difficulties of life. Perhaps they think it's really nobody's business, that it's a personal choice. But honestly, it's a slippery slope to a slimy pit.

1. **We all start on equal ground.**
   - According to Romans 1:18-20, *what* things are evident and clearly seen?

   - *Where* and *how* are they evident and clearly seen?

   - So where does that leave the person who chooses to seek fulfillment through ungodly habits? (Hint: see the end of verse 20.)

2. **We set ourselves on a slippery slope when we don't acknowledge God properly.**
   - What is the first wrong step taken in Romans 1:21?

   - And so what happens in their minds and hearts as a result?

3. **We take a dangerous step on that slippery slope when we confuse things.**
   - What foolish mistake is made in Romans 1:22-23?

   - Exactly what exchange have they made at this point (vs. 23)? Be specific.

- And so what is God's response (vs. 24)?

- Is that fair? Why or why not? (Think back to #1)

4. **We then take a second dangerous step on that slippery slope and begin a fast descent.**
- What is the second exchange made in vs. 25?

- And now what do they worship and serve (vs. 25)?

- And so what is God's response (vs. 26)?

- And what exchange is made in verses 26-27? (Keep in mind that this passage describes the slippery slope into homosexuality, *one type* of co-dependent relationship, but the pattern applies to other types of idolatrous relationships as well – alcoholism, incessant shopping, pornography, gluttony, you name it.)

5. **Once we've slid down the slippery slope, we can no longer just easily "step off of it" even if we give it our best try.**
- Now, in verse 28, what is their attitude toward God?

- And what is God's response in verse 28?

- According to verses 29 through 31, what are they now *filled* with?

- And as the final thud of hitting rock bottom on this slippery slope, what is their attitude toward their sin in verse 32?

- Lest we think "that's just not fair," what do these who now dwell at the bottom of their slippery pit know to be true according to verse 32?

Sweet friend, I don't mean to scare or threaten you. But we all need to agree that you don't just suddenly end up at the bottom of a pit, at least not at the bottom of one that is of your own making.

I've been in a few pits and at the time I didn't want to take responsibility for any of them. Looking back I can trace every slippery inch down the slope and see how it corresponds to the biblical pattern in Romans 1. By the time I landed with a thud at the bottom I was making excuses for my behavior and rationalizing why it was ok. And to make myself even more comfortable in my pit, I would look for others who were living the same way, caught in the same addiction (though I would never call it that) and condone their behavior as well.

Not all of my learned behaviors ended up all the way at the bottom of such pits. Sometimes, as in the case of my bout with bulimia, God mercifully jerked me by the arm out of the pit while I was still on the descent. As I rubbed my aching shoulder, so to speak, I looked down at the slimy bottom of that hole with disgust and gratitude. God did not have to save me that way, but in those instances He graciously chose to.

Has God ever miraculously delivered you from a slippery slope you were on? Tell me about it.

There have been a few times when I did hit rock bottom. And this is why point number five is so important to understand. When I, by my own stubbornness and disobedience, made it all the way to the bottom of a pit, there was no climbing out with my own two hands. I needed help.

Not only did I have to depend completely on the help of God, throwing myself at His mercy through earnest repentance and willing cooperation, but I had to seek professional assistance at times. Not always in the form of a counselor, mind you. Sometimes I simply needed the wise counsel of a good book that provided biblical principles which functioned like rungs of a ladder so I could climb out one step at a time. Other times I did need to arrange for accountability with another strong believer who would hold on tight when I began to slip back downwards. And then there were times I sought professional counsel. Don't be ashamed or afraid or too proud to ask for help. Sometimes there is simply no other way back to solid ground.

But let's end this week's study on a more positive note. Think back over Romans 1:18-32 and answer a few thought provoking questions. Feel free to make application to your own situations as you see fit. That's the best way to make this study work for you.

1. What would have prevented one from starting down the slippery slope to begin with? What could the person have been doing *right* so they never would have chosen the *wrong* path?

2. What are some of the things (we've used them as examples over and over this week) for which we sometimes "exchange the natural function for that which is unnatural?" In other words, give examples of things that are actually good or ok, but we abuse them by trying to gain something from them that they were never meant to deliver.

3. Did you notice that in the end the person who has slipped all the way down the slope is indeed *full* of something? You might have thought they would be completely empty, but notice they had set out to be *filled* and they were. What does that tell you about the deceptive nature of coping devices and learned behaviors?

⌒办⌒

Summary

Well done, sweet sister. You've worked hard this week and I've undoubtedly worn you out. I hope this tough and time-consuming unit hasn't scared you off. We had some rough ground to cover, but I believe it was necessary for three reasons:
1. To alert you to the serious consequences of trying to find nourishment for our souls in other places besides Jesus Christ
2. To uncover some of the unhealthy and unholy coping mechanisms many of us are using to deal with our unsatisfied longings
3. To increase your appetite for the bread which endures to eternal life and the water that springs up in you like a fountain so you never thirst again

Please join me next week as we finally begin to learn how to feast on the Bread of Life, to drink from the Living Water. It will be so worth it!

I am supplying you with a brief list of helpful resources for overcoming addictions and co-dependencies. If you know of other valuable resources, please share them with your discussion group.

Helpful Resources for Overcoming Codependency

Celebrate Recovery – This is a Christ-centered recovery program that helps people struggling with hurts, habits and hang-ups by showing them the loving power of Jesus Christ through a recovery process. You can locate a CR program in your area by visiting their website at www.celebraterecovery.com.

Cloud, Henry, and John Townsend. *Boundaries*. Grand Rapids: Zondervan, 1992.

Moore, Beth. *Get Out of That Pit*. Nashville, Tennessee: Thomas Nelson Publisher, 2007.

Week 2
Discussion Questions

1. Have you noticed a correlation between your attitudes, words, and actions and the degree to which your soul feels full and satisfied? How does soul dissatisfaction tend to manifest itself in your behavior?

2. How are you affected when life requires a lot from you but you have little to give because you're on "empty"? In other words, how do you react when your employer, husband, children, friends, etc. need more from you than you feel you can give?

3. How did Paul's words in Philippians 2:3-4, discussed at the end of Day 1, encourage and instruct you?

4. At what point does something that is initially good and wholesome become an idol? What qualifies something as an idol?

5. Why do you think Jesus brought up the Samaritan woman's marital state and her relationships with men when He was talking with her at the well? If He were talking with you at the well, what would He ask you about?

6. If a friend asked you what it means to be co-dependent, how would you answer her? How would you define a co-dependent relationship between two people?

7. Thinking back to the slippery slope detailed in Romans 1:18-32, what are some keys to staying off of this dangerous slope and avoiding the pit it leads to?

8. Share some of the sources for help that you or others close to you have used to successfully get out of a pit of addiction (i.e., food addictions, substance abuse, codependent relationships, overspending, etc.). What do these resources seem to have in common?

Week 3 – Eat What is Good

I went to the same dentist year after year when I was growing up. I've never enjoyed going to the dentist, but Dr. Snow had a way of making those dreaded cleanings and fillings a little more bearable. After your appointment the receptionist would hand you a small slip of paper with a signed note from Dr. Snow that entitled you to one ice cream cone at the drugstore just a few doors down. (I've just dated myself by telling you they still served ice cream at the drugstore!) I always thought it was a little strange to have your teeth cleaned or your cavity filled only to head straight to the drugstore for some milky sugar. But I didn't let that stop me from taking that slip of paper straight to the ice cream counter.

Today I feel like I should offer you a signed note entitling you to some delectable delight of your choice as well, since last week's homework may have felt somewhat like a root canal to you. But while I can't give you a scoop of your favorite ice cream, I can offer you a swivel seat at the counter. You see, this week we finally get to learn how to eat from the Bread of Life, how to drink gustily from the Living Water.

So take your seat, lick your lips with anticipation, and take a whiff of what's cooking. You're in for a treat!

Day 1
Choosing to Eat Well

As I begin writing this session of the Bible study, I am enjoying a creamy, sweet piece of chocolate from a tiny box of Whitman's candies my husband put on my desk a few days ago. I have to admit, it is delicious. But I will be a good girl and eat only one right now. Otherwise, I will spoil my appetite for dinner when I am much more likely to eat something a little healthier.

I don't always choose so wisely. Sometimes I indulge in unhealthy, sugary snacks and treats to the point that I can almost feel my heart racing. When I eat an especially fatty meal, I enjoy it at the time but later I tend to become lethargic. I can almost feel the cholesterol settle in my arteries. And as I get older, I have to be a little more diligent about not eating spicy foods or things laden with caffeine late in the evening. Otherwise I don't sleep well.

Just like we have to make responsible and wise decisions about what we eat, we also have to consciously choose how we will satisfy our soul hungers.

You'll remember last week we read in Isaiah about idolatry and God's people forsaking Him. In the passages in Isaiah, God is speaking through the prophet to His people to rebuke them for their unfaithfulness. He points out their waywardness and then spells out the consequences of their actions. They had turned from a faithful and loving God to seek satisfaction from lifeless idols, foreign nations, pagan gods, and silly rituals. They had not feasted on His Word, but chose instead to eat the poisonous but sweet tasting words of their lying priests.

But still, throughout this long book of God's stern judgment upon His people, His love and mercy remain steadfast.

Please read Isaiah 30:18 in your Bible. What is God's attitude toward His wayward people according to this scripture?

Who is blessed according to this verse?

Last week we established that many of us, like the people of Israel, have committed idolatry by running to other sources with our soul hungers. We have sought fulfillment through other things, people, and experiences instead of resting in God's promise to provide everything we need or desire. God does not take lightly our idolatry. He takes it as a personal offense, because it is such. But He also graciously reaches out to those who return to Him with passionate repentance and longing hearts.

Today we begin our reading in Isaiah 55 where God is offering once again to bless His people. If they will return to Him with a hunger and thirst for His goodness, then He will completely satisfy them.

Please carefully read Isaiah 55:1-13 in your Bible. Then answer the following questions.

1. Who does God invite to come to Him in verse 1?

2. How does He tell them to come?

3. In verse 2, what does God say the people have been doing?

4. Have you been "spending money" for that which does not really satisfy? Explain.

5. In verse 2, what does God instruct and invite His children to do?

6. Summarize verses 6 and 7. What does God want His wayward child to do? When? What will be the results?

7. What does God expect His wayward child to recognize according to verses 8-9?

8. According to the familiar scriptures in Isaiah 55:10-11, what happens when God speaks?

9. What will be the final result for the child who returns to the Lord hungry and thirsty for what only He can give, according to Isaiah 55:12-13?

If you have realized that you have sought fulfillment from an idol of your own making rather than depending exclusively upon God for satisfaction, then you are invited back to the King's table. He still has a seat for you and will welcome you back without condemnation. He simply requests that you completely abandon whatever empty, broken cisterns you have been visiting and come to His table with a hearty appetite. Bring your empty water jar with you and put it on the table with expectation. He will fill it to overflowing.

In so many ways, life is a matter of choices. God will not force Himself upon us, even though it must surely pain Him to stand back and wait for our voluntary response at times. He loves us and greatly desires to meet every need that He created within us. But we must choose to let Him do so.

Today I simply encourage you to choose to dine at the King's table. If you recognize that you have been "spending money for what is not bread and your wages for what does not satisfy," then make a choice today to stop. Come instead to the One who invites you to "eat what is good, and delight yourself in abundance." Not only that, but reminiscent of Jesus' words in John 6, He invites you to come with no money at all in hand. There is no charge for this abundant feast.

Please write out Isaiah 55:2 in the space below, using whatever translation you are comfortable memorizing from.

With the mention of "memorizing," some of you are shaking in your boots right now. Shake all you want, but I'm going to encourage you to go with me on this concept.

During the next two weeks we will be putting together a step by step plan for how to eat the Bread of Life so that our hungers will be satisfied. We will be learning very practical and doable steps for drinking the Living Water so that it not only quenches our thirsts, but overflows from us as well. Part of that plan hinges on knowing some key scriptures that will keep us securely in our seats at the King's table and prevent us from wandering off in the direction of those broken cisterns again. You just read in Isaiah 55:10-11 that God's Word will accomplish in you what He purposes to accomplish. I believe that, but I also believe the extent to which His Word changes and grows you is in direct proportion to the degree you take it in.

I want you to try your very best to begin memorizing these selected scriptures with me over the next few weeks. It's not easy for me either and I don't always get every word of the scripture connected to the right reference; however, I spend enough time working on memorizing that over time the scripture definitely does its powerful work in my life, even if I never recite it perfectly. And, no, I do not expect you to have these memorized by the end of this short study. But hopefully you will continue to meditate on them and memorize them in the coming months.

1. **Purchase a plastic 4x6 photo album**, one of those inexpensive ones you can usually get at a discount type store for a bargain. Also **get a small package of 4x6 index cards**.

2. **Write the memory verse in the translation of your choice on an index card**. Put the scripture reference in the top left corner and a summarizing subject title in the top right corner.

Isaiah 55:2   **Eat What is Good**

Why do you spend money for what is not bread, and your wages for what does not satisfy? Listen carefully to Me, and eat what is good, and delight yourself in abundance.

---

3. **Put your index card in your photo album**. Keep it somewhere handy so you can refer to it several times a day. Mine usually stays in my kitchen so I can look over my scriptures in the morning during my quiet time, while I eat lunch, when I'm waiting on the pasta water to boil at dinner, or after I've finished the dishes at night. I also take my album with me on business trips and vacations, and it often accompanies me on walks so I can exercise my body and my brain at the same time.

4. **Focus on each scripture for a full week**. I'm going to be giving you several each week, but you can take your time learning them. Read the scripture slowly and purposefully, thinking about the meaning as you read. Meditate on the scripture by slowly applying it to your own life. Then begin memorizing one phrase at a time.

5. **Try to read over your scriptures several times a day**. Storing God's Word in your heart takes effort. It does not come easily or quickly to most of us. In fact, anything

done easily and quickly is rarely worth as much as that which takes greater diligence. Make meditating on and memorizing scripture a priority and it will pay huge dividends in your life.

One more thing. If you already have a similar system for memorizing scripture, that's great. I just want to encourage you to put these cards for this study in a separate album, at least for now. Like I said, we will be using these memory verses as building blocks for our step by step plan for feasting on the Bread of Life and it's important that you see how they work together to accomplish that purpose in your life.

So what are you waiting for? I truly hope you'll join me in this long-term assignment. Unless you welcome the accountability, I won't ask you to recite your scriptures to anyone. But stored deep in your heart they will speak loudly to you during those moments when your soul aches with hunger. So get that first index card and write Isaiah 55:2 on it. It's time to return to the King's table and eat what is good.

Day 2
Just Give Me the How-To!

Well it's time to get to the practical nitty gritty of the matter. We've established that Jesus is the Bread of Life and that He offers to feed us that which will endure to eternal life, that which satisfies those deep, eternal longings. In John chapter 4 He offered the Samaritan woman living water that would quench her thirst permanently. We know Jesus is the one who can satisfy our every soul desire, but how?

Even as we quickly review the two steps we learned for feasting on the Bread of Life in week one of this study, we come up short on details.

Do you remember the two directives Jesus gave in John 6 that we identified as the two steps for ordering from "Jesus' Soul Food Menu?" Look up the corresponding scriptures only if you need your memory jogged.

    1. _____ in Jesus. (John 6:29)

    2. _____ to Jesus. (John 6:35)

We determined that Jesus acknowledges our soul needs, is not turned off by them, and even desires to meet them. Just like He voluntarily fed the crowd fish and bread until they were completely satisfied, He longs to take care of our hungers as well. In order to receive that sustaining "meal" from Him, we simply need to *believe* in Him and *come* to Him. We must believe He is who He says He is and that He can and will do all He promises. Then we need to turn away from any other source of provision and completely depend on Him, coming to Him alone for that which will satisfy.

But as much as I believe we need to nail down these concepts firmly in our minds and hearts, I also believe most of us need something more. At this point we have what I often call a "good Sunday school theory." We know the teaching of God's Word on this subject and we know His Word is a reliable source for all truth. But it would be beneficial to know how to work it out in practical, everyday terms. We must test the theory over and over like good scientists, not so we can determine *if* the theory is reliable, but so we will begin *to believe* with 100% assurance that it is indeed more than a theory; it is fact. Only then will we begin to live this principle out on a daily basis in a way that bears consistent fruit in our lives. That is my goal. I don't just want to know the truths of God's Word; I want to live them out with victory every day.

Also, while I can literally believe in Jesus, I can't literally walk up to Him, hold out my hand or my empty water jar, and ask Him to feed me. So how do I come to Him for my soul needs?

One reason I believe we so often go to the idols we mentioned last week instead of going to Jesus for our soul needs is that at least the idols are physically accessible and visible. They may have skin on, they may be found in a bottle, or they may be encountered through an experience, but somehow we can lay our hands on them and probably even see them with our eyes. While we won't be able, aside from an unusual encounter, to lay our hands or our eyes on the Messiah, we can, in time, begin to see the results of going to Him with our needs. But we must hone our spiritual vision so we are looking for and acknowledging Jesus' involvement in our lives. Only then will we recognize that He is the one providing our needs and, thus, attribute our fullness to Him alone.

And so, without further ado, we begin that process today. Over the next two weeks, beginning today, I will walk you through eight steps for feasting on the Bread of Life. Based on biblical principles and scriptures, these steps will give you practical actions to take so you begin to "eat" only what is good instead of that which does not satisfy.

Step One – Invite Jesus to Work in Your Life

It has occurred to me that up to this point I have addressed you as one who already knows Jesus the Messiah intimately. I have assumed that while you may not be feasting on the Bread of Life, you do at least know Him *as* the Bread of Life. But I cannot afford to make that assumption any longer.

Please describe your relationship with Jesus Christ. Give as much detail as possible.

I hope your description included mention of a time when you came to God, confessed your sinfulness, admitted your need for a savior, and accepted God's free gift of salvation through Jesus Christ. The very first thing we need from the Bread of Life is our salvation, and He alone can provide that.

Perhaps you have heard people speak of "asking Jesus into their hearts." What exactly does that mean?

Please read Psalm 66:5 in your Bible. What invitation does the Psalmist give?

God is at work all around us, and all He does benefits us greatly. He is an involved and active God. Perhaps you have seen God at work around you and that is one of the things that piqued your interest in studying about Him through the Bible. He wants to do more than just work around us. He wants to work *in* us. He desires to be in a personal relationship with us so that He can be more than just a distant God whom we admire or fear from afar. Only when He has been granted full access to your heart can He meet those soul needs we've discussed in this study. He longs to be actively involved in our lives. Unfortunately, one barrier stands in the way.

Please read Romans 3:23 in your Bible.

The Bible tells us that every person has sinned. There is not a single exception. We sin when we do or say anything that goes contrary to the character or ways of God. He is completely good, loving, gracious, right, and just. When we do not heed His standards for living and instead do things our way and live independently of Him, we sin. That sin, even just one, separates us from our holy God.

Whether this is a review for you or a brand new introduction to some life-changing scriptures, please read the following passages in your Bible and summarize each with one short sentence.

John 1:29 –

John 3:16-17–

Romans 5:8 –

Romans 6:23 –

Jesus took care of our sin problem. He was the only one who could. He is God in the flesh. He lived among men and faced temptation, yet never once sinned. Therefore, because He did not owe the penalty for sin, He could pay for ours. And He did. When Jesus died on the cross and shed His blood, His death paid the price for our sinfulness and His blood acted as atonement for our sins. In other words, His blood washed away the very record of our sin. And now, without the stain of sin, we can have a perfect, intimate relationship with God, both now and forever.

Still, God does not force this sin solution upon anyone. We must voluntarily and humbly admit that we are sinners who need the atoning work of Jesus. We have to ask Him to apply His blood to our lives and accept it as a free, unearned gift. We have to realize that this gift was His idea and that it is given out of love and grace.

Please read Titus 3:5-7 and Ephesians 2:8-9 in your Bible.

We also must understand that in accepting this gift of grace, we willingly enter into a covenant relationship with God. He has redeemed us from the penalty of sin and we have given Him rightful ownership of us. We belong to Him. That means we quit calling the shots in our lives and agree to make Jesus our master instead. He becomes our Lord and we commit to obey Him.

Please read Romans 6:22 and 1 Corinthians 6:20.

If you have never accepted God's free gift of salvation through Jesus Christ, I encourage you to do that today. You can trust Jesus to be your Savior and your Lord by saying a heartfelt and sincere prayer similar to this one:

Dear God,
I want You to work in my life. I admit I am a sinner and have been living independently of You. Please forgive me. Thank You for allowing Jesus to die for my sins. I know He has risen and conquered death for me. I invite You to be the Lord of my life and begin a new work in me. Thank You for coming into my life. In Jesus' name, amen.

If you chose to pray this prayer or a similar one today, welcome to the family of God! I encourage you to share this decision with someone immediately, preferably a believer who can give you more information about Jesus and how to grow in your relationship with Him. Actually, continuing in this Bible study is a great start to that relationship. But the good news is that we don't need to have all the answers about Jesus right now, nor do we have to clean up our lives in order to start this new relationship with Him. The Bible teaches that the Holy Spirit, God's very presence, moves into our lives and takes up residence when we are saved. He then takes on the responsibility for perfecting us into Christ's image.

Please read 2 Corinthians 5:17 and Philippians 1:6 in your Bible. What can and will God do now?

Yes, God is at work around us. But He also longs to be at work in us. Whether you have been a follower of Jesus saved by grace for years and years or you just asked Jesus to take over today, I encourage you to give Him permission to do a new work in your life. Only then will you begin to see and feel Him satisfying your soul hungers.

Please write a simple prayer asking Jesus to be at work in your life. Ask Him to help you notice His activity and to feel His presence.

Finally, let's add a scripture to our memory book, one that reminds us that God alone can and will completely satisfy us, but only within the confines of our relationship with Jesus Christ.

Please read Philippians 4:19 in your Bible and write it on a 4 x 6 index card to be added to your booklet. In the top right corner of the card, label this scripture "Satisfied in Christ."

⌒᷄⌒

Day 3
Step 2 – Evaluate Your Current Diet

As I write today's session, it is the beginning of a new year and we have just enjoyed another Christmas season. In the months leading up to Christmas I had made a concentrated effort to improve my eating habits. I was eating more fiber, less fat, less sugar, and more fruits and vegetables. But as Thanksgiving turned into Christmas and Christmas continued on and then Christmas turned into my wedding anniversary, I strayed further and further from that healthy diet.

When I noticed I wasn't feeling as energetic or quite as light on my feet, literally, I decided it was time to re-evaluate how I was eating. For instance, over the holidays I had gotten into a delicious but fattening habit of eating a huge bagel with cream cheese every morning for breakfast. (I fear that many of you are shaking your heads in disgust right now. I beg you; please don't hold this weakness against me.) Last week, as I prepared to go to the grocery store, I looked in my pantry and noticed I had only one bagel left. I had a decision to make. Would I buy more bagels and cream cheese or would I switch to a healthy cereal with skim milk? This may sound like an elementary decision for most of you, especially if you are over thirty-five and your metabolism has come to a screeching halt as mine has. But I honestly struggled with this decision. Not only did I have to come to terms with what I had been eating, but I had to judge accurately the affect the diet was having on me. Sure, those bagels slathered in cream cheese were making my taste buds happy at breakfast, but they were also making my hips wider and my cholesterol count higher. Plus, being low in fiber and high in sugar, the bagels weren't keeping me full and satisfied throughout the morning like I needed them to. If I wanted to eat in a healthy way that satisfied my hunger but also kept my body healthy and energetic, I would need to make some changes; thus, no more bagels.

Have you put our first memory verse on an index card and placed it in your scripture memory album? I hope so, but if not I encourage you to do so soon. Let's review that first scripture together.

Read aloud Isaiah 55:2, either from your Bible or your index card, *three times*.
On what does God accuse His people of spending their money and their hard earned wages? (Check all that apply.)

_____ Food that is good for them

_____ That which is not bread

_____ Healthy sustenance

_____ That which satisfies

_____ That which leaves them hungry

Keep in mind that Isaiah is speaking figuratively. God's people have been spending their money, figuratively speaking, for what is not bread, figuratively speaking. They have been working hard and paying the price for those things which do not satisfy their souls.

In contrast, what does God offer them? (Check all that apply.)

_____ That which is beneficial to them

_____ That which *tastes* good but spoils their appetites

_____ Healthy sustenance

_____ Something they can really sink their teeth into, something to delight in

_____ A little bit of something to tide them over

_____ Abundance, more than enough

_____ Something that's good for them but doesn't taste great

Obviously I departed a little from the wording of the scripture and included some interpretation in the list above, but I hope my choices gave you something to think about. Let's look at that word *satisfy* because it seems to be a key word in this scripture.

Using whatever dictionaries you have available, define the words *satisfy* and *satisfied*.

Satisfy –

Satisfied –

The Hebrew word translated *satisfy* is *sobah* and comes from the Hebrew word *saba*, which means "satisfied, sated, surfeited." This word is used approximately 96 times in the Hebrew Old Testament. I'd say that's significant usage. While many times the word refers to actually being fed and satisfied through eating or grazing, in the case of cattle or sheep, even those uses are often symbolic references to God's abundant and satisfying provision for His people.

To be satisfied means to have one's desires, expectations, requirements or demands fulfilled. To truly satisfy means to put an end to a hunger or craving through sufficient or ample provision. It means to cause one to be completely content because their hunger has been sated or their thirst has been quenched. If one is satisfied then there are no other needs, longings, desires, or empty places.

When we think of being satisfied, we may think of having one need completely met but other lingering desires that have yet to be fulfilled. But when God satisfies us, He satisfies completely. No other person or thing or experience can satisfy our every need or desire. Only God can satisfy to that degree.

Read the following scriptures and note *how* or *to what extent* God satisfies.

Psalm 81:16

Psalm 91:16Psalm 103:1, 5

Psalm 104:24-28

Psalm 145:15-16

When God satisfies our hungers, He does so with *good* things. He never gives us what seems satisfactory but is indeed harmful, deficient, dangerous, or empty. He meets our soul needs generously, abundantly, healthily, and with only the finest.

So the leading question is what source have you been going to, besides God, for satisfaction? Whatever it is, I can guarantee you by the authority of God's Word that it does not satisfy the way God does, completely and without lacking. You may, in fact probably do, find temporary satisfaction from various things, people, or experiences. But the type of satisfaction offered by anything or anyone else can only be temporary and partial at best, harmful, dangerous, and unhealthy at worst.

By this point in the study you should have performed enough self-examination to be able to identify where you have been going for satisfaction. I encourage you to reflect on your list of favorite empty cistern choices that apply to your situation. Honest reflection removes any deception that would prevent you from allowing God to meet your needs.

It's time to consider again the soul hungers and longings that seem to specifically drive us the most and to honestly name how we have been trying to satisfy those desires. Just like I opened my pantry door and took a long hard look at those bagels I'd been eating for breakfast, we need to accurately and honestly assess what we've been filling our lives with. I'll admit, when I looked at that last bagel and began making my grocery list for the next week, I began justifying why it wouldn't hurt to buy more. I even searched the nutritional label, hoping to find some redeeming quality. But if I wanted to eat food that was both satisfying and healthy for me I knew I had to give up the bagels and choose something better, something very different.

If you find yourself trying to justify some source of "satisfaction" that you've been eating from, the search for a redeeming quality should indicate to you that you've been spending your money for what is not food. Don't play games here, I beg you. Be real. God knows the truth about what you've been eating for soul satisfaction. You might as well agree with Him and call it what it is.

One more thing. As we evaluate our current "diet" we're going to list everything we've been "eating," not just the toxic, fattening, unhealthy stuff. Hopefully, you have some healthy relationships that partially satisfy. More than likely you have a number of appropriate experiences that bring you some degree of satisfaction. And you may even have a thing or two in your possession that gives you appropriate fulfillment. List those too, by all means. We don't need to condemn ourselves into believing that everything in our lives up to this point has been unhealthy for us. We might need to re-label some of those people, experiences, or things with truthful information. And we might need to limit our consumption of some of them. But we don't necessarily need to throw out everything in our pantries. So for now, just list what you've been "eating." Try not to label things as good or bad yet. Just write down what's in your pantry – what you've been going to in order to have your soul hungers satisfied.

Each circle on the next page is a dinner plate that represents a specific perceived soul hunger you have. Yours will be different from mine or your girlfriend's. Yours may be different today than they were ten years ago.

1. **At the top of each plate, name one soul hunger that seems to drive you.** Think carefully about these. What is it you long for? What does your soul hunger for? You might want to look back to Week 1, Day 2 to get started, but don't limit yourself to what you marked there. We've covered a lot of ground since then. You do not have to use all of the plates, but I suggest you try to name all of your plates or hungers before you proceed to step 2.

2. **On the plates, name the people, things, or experiences you have gone to for satisfaction of that particular soul hunger.** Remember, these are not all necessarily

"bad." Just list everywhere you've gone to have that need met. If privacy is an issue, simply use initials or code words of some sort. I encourage you to list anything and everything you have ever gone to for fulfillment, even if it is not a daily practice. An exhaustive list will be more beneficial to you in the days to come than one that *looks right*. We need to be very real about where we've been for satisfaction, even if we know better.

Example: *Companionship.*

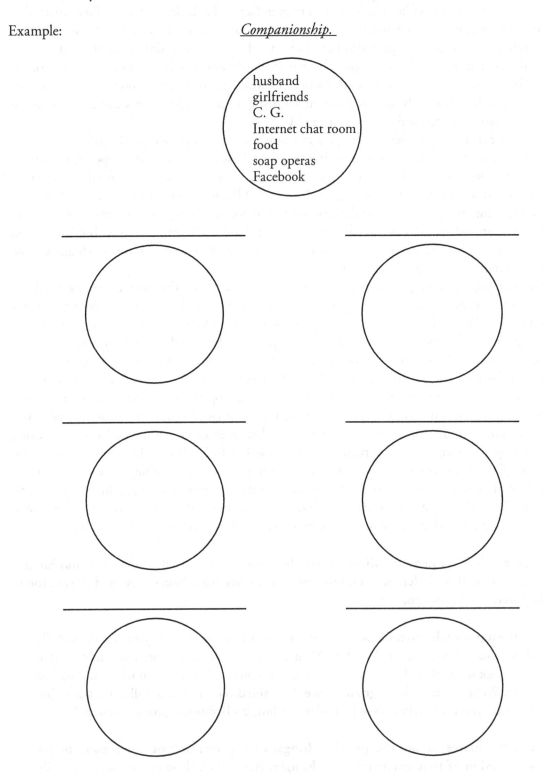

husband
girlfriends
C. G.
Internet chat room
food
soap operas
Facebook

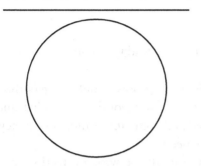 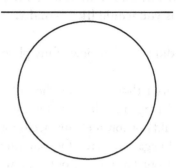

Good job, friends! I know that was hard work. It was for me also. Tomorrow we will look at each of the "items" on our plates a little more closely, evaluating their health value, where they belong in our "diet," and whether or not they should remain in our pantry. But for today, let's celebrate the fact that wherever we've allowed our soul hungers to drive us, we have a God who is waiting anxiously to satisfy every desire with *good* stuff. We have a God who invites us to come to Him with no money in hand, heed His life-changing words, and delight ourselves in His abundant provision. And we're well on our way to learning how to eat consistently from His bounteous table.

Day 4
Step 3 – Sort Out Your Pantry, Part 1

I detest cleaning out my refrigerator. Sure, every now and again I enjoy the purging effects of tossing a few leftovers or overripe vegetables in order to make more space for newer, fresher groceries. But poking my head deep into the fridge, pulling everything out, examining expiration labels, opening jar lids to smell and inspect the contents, and wiping everything down? Yuck!

That is why I feel a little bad about today's assignment. But friend, if we're going to learn to eat the Bread of Life, that which truly satisfies like nothing else can, we'll have to do the hard work of cleaning out some things first. There's simply no way around it. So if it helps, we'll think of it as cleaning out our pantries rather than our refrigerators. That seems a little less daunting to me.

We're going to take two days to sort out the things from which we have been trying to satisfy our soul hungers. Today we will set the standards for what we may need to toss from our pantries. We'll define that which is unhealthy, toxic, dangerous, or unfulfilling by the standards set forth in God's Word. Tomorrow we will determine what kinds of healthy relationships, things, and experiences can stay in our pantry. But we'll also apply new labels to those so that we understand the quantities we may consume and in which situations they are appropriate.

Let's begin by reviewing the plates you set up yesterday. Look back over the hungers with which you labeled each plate. Do you need to add a soul hunger that you identified since completing the last lesson? Then look back over the contents of those plates. Has the Lord revealed any other people, things, or experiences you are drawing from in order to have your soul hungers satisfied?

Take a few minutes to look over the plates you created on Day 2 and make any additions or corrections you would like to make.

_____ I did a quick review of my plates and made any necessary adjustments.

For years I thought I was the only one who had these deep down soul hungers that seemed insatiable. I longed for Jesus to be my all and all, the center of my world, but I didn't understand how He could possibly meet my needs for purpose, significance, companionship, or intimacy, among others. So I began to search for something to satisfy these needs.

It turns out I'm not the only one who has been driven in all the wrong directions by my soul hungers. In fact, God's Word describes many such pursuits of the soul. It also tells us what went wrong in each case.

Today we will look at a number of scriptures straight from the ancient pages of God's Word that shed light on some of the places where we've been spending money for what does not satisfy, where we've been working for and buying that which is not bread at all. We'll allow these scriptures to help us categorize some of the relationships, things, and experiences on our plates. While not everything on our plates will fail the scrutiny of these passages, we must be willing to take the lids off, check the labels carefully, and truthfully examine each item with which we've loaded our plates.

Please read the scriptures in the following entries *before* you read the name I have given that particular food group and my explanation of the types of things that fall into that category.
- Read each scripture and mark the word *satisfy* or any of its variations in your Bible.
- Note what you find about being satisfied or not finding satisfaction.
- Read my comments and see if you agree with my assessment of the "food" mentioned in those scriptures and how that food shows up in our "diets."
- Write the name I've given that food group in the blank I've provided.
- List any food that is in *your diet* that would fall into that category.

1. _____

- Esther 5:9-14 ("avails me nothing" = doesn't satisfy)

- Habakkuk 2:5

- This food is that with which we try to fill our souls but is evasive and elusive. It is like sugar that tastes sweet to the tongue, but disintegrates quickly in your mouth and never really makes you feel full; therefore, I've titled it *Cotton Candy*. It is that dress on the mannequin, that magical number on the scales, that vacation advertised on television in which the whole family is happy and having a great time. It may be a glass of wine that leads to another, or a cookie that is followed by three more. And, as in the case of Haman in Esther 5, it may be accolades, promotions or revenge. It simply holds more appeal to the eye than it does substance to the soul.

- Foods from your plates that fall into this category:

2. _____

- Proverbs 6:29-35

- Deuteronomy 23:24-25

- This category is full of things, people, and even experiences that we take for ourselves even though they don't really belong to us. In fact, they probably belong to someone else, but we take them to satisfy our own needs selfishly. Sometimes these "foods" have been offered to us generously by someone else – such as their time, their friendship, their home, their good favor – but we have taken more than is appropriate and healthy. Things like adultery, shoplifting, embezzlement, tax evasion, and robbery fall into this category obviously, but so do smaller offenses such as manipulation tactics, abuse of generosity, etc. I've called this category *Stolen Candy* because these things are sometimes given in good trust and then gobbled up greedily, but they're also often stolen outright.

- Foods from your plates that fall into this category:

3. _____

- Ecclesiastes 1:8

- Ecclesiastes 4:8

- Ecclesiastes 5:10

- Ezekiel 7:19-20

- These are things we believe are *supposed to be* filling to us. In many cases our culture has told us these things fulfill and we have believed it, but we're left wondering why we still feel empty even though we have plenty. Often these things are obtained through either dishonest or shady means or they are acquired through too much – too much money (putting us in debt), too much of our time, too much sacrifice, too much work. This category is also full of things that have been elevated to a higher purpose than they are meant to serve. These are things that are good, serviceable and even necessary, such as food, work, possessions, etc., but we have given them greater value than they are meant to have in our lives. So I've called this category *Deceptive Packaging* because you rarely get what you "paid for."

- Foods from your plates that fall into this category:

4. _____

- Proverbs 27:20

- Isaiah 9:18-21

- Amos 4:6-8

- These scriptures describe our tendency to want what is on someone else's plate, not because we really want or need it, but because they have it and it *seems* to satisfy them. This category is built on envy and jealousy. It includes our pursuit of fulfillment through what appears to work for someone else. For instance, I decide that I'll be happier if my husband starts bringing me coffee in bed in the mornings because I find out my girlfriend's husband does that for her. Or I believe I'll be more fulfilled as a woman if I go back to work and put my children in daycare, not because I need to financially, but because all my friends have and they *seem* happier than me. I call this category of "food" *What She's Having.*

- Foods from your plates that fall into this category:

5. _____

- Haggai 1:2-11

- Matthew 5:6; 6:31-34

- In both of these scriptures we see our tendency to seek fulfillment through misguided priorities. Out of our desire to feed our flesh, we put God and His kingdom further down our priority list and we seek fulfillment of our own needs first. From these scriptures we learn a powerful lesson. If we seek God and His kingdom agenda, He will satisfy our soul needs and we won't have to. This category includes anything you are seeking passionately above and before Him. These are not necessarily bad things, but you have put them before God. I call these "foods" *Dessert First.*

- Foods from your plates that fall into this category:

6. _____

- Ecclesiastes 6:1-9

- Hosea 13:4-6

- This category is a little harder to detect because it includes those things that God has graciously blessed us with out of love and out of His promise to provide. But these things, people, and experiences have become more important to us than the One who gave them, not what He intended at all. The danger in being blessed with much is that those blessings, instead of the God who blessed us with them, can become the desires of our heart. Thus, instead of developing a relationship with the Giver of all good and perfect gifts (James 1:17), we fixate on the gifts themselves, demanding more of them and hinging our satisfaction on them. I call this category *Fast Food* because it is as though we want to take what God gives us and dash off greedily with it instead of saying thank you and sitting down to build a real relationship with the One who has given so generously. Instead of appreciating and being drawn to His generosity, we concentrate on the gift and look to it to satisfy our soul.

- Foods from your plates that fall into this category:

7. _____

- Genesis 12:1-9; 25:8 (This is the first biblical mention of a person being *satisfied*.)

- Psalm 107:4-9

- Matthew 5:6

- Matthew 14:20

- Finally, the *Bread of Life*. This category contains all of those spiritual blessings that really make life enjoyable and fulfilling – God's peace, His presence, the joy of the Lord, His Word, a transformed life, forgiveness, His grace, and more. But it also includes those things that He blesses us with and we appropriate as just that – blessings. Things like a long healthy life, food for our tables, homes to live in and transportation to get us where we need to be. This category is full of things that always seem to be plenty, enough, satisfying, even though it might not look to others that we have so much. Why? Because when we look at these blessings correctly we realize God has been good in giving us our daily bread and we need no more. We don't try to hoard these items, but enjoy them with satisfaction each day.

- Foods from your plates that fall into this category:

Oh sweet friend (I hope we're still friends!), you have worked hard today. I will not bother you with even one more instruction. I simply hope you will continue to ponder the revelation we have discovered in God's Word today. It's a lot to digest, I know. You can take off your apron and go sit down for a while, even put your feet up. But I hope you'll let God continue to speak to you about anything in your "pantry" that you haven't quite found a place for yet. Let's make sure we have clean pantries by the end of this week.

cu

Day 5
Step 3 – Sort Out Your Pantry, Part II

Tie that apron back on, sweet friend; we have work to do. We're still in the messy and tiresome process of sorting out our "food pantries" from which we've tried to satisfy our soul hungers in the past. As I mentioned on Day 3, we need to closely examine and properly label every relationship, thing, and experience we may have ever gone to for fulfillment. I hope you're not hiding anything in the back of your pantry that you'd just rather not deal with. Sometimes I do that when I'm cleaning out my kitchen pantry, but I know if I want God to do a real and lasting work in my life through a Bible study, I'd better put everything out on the table so He and I can honestly assess it.

Please look back over Days 3 and 4 and see if you need to add anything to your plates or if you need to re-label something that is already on your plates by putting it in the appropriate category from our list on Day 4.

_____ I've checked my plates from Day 3 and the categories from Day 4 and everything is now where it needs to be.

Three Specific Types of "Food" to Flush Down the Drain

Now I want to introduce to you three specific types of foods which are based on the first six food groups and need to be completely eliminated from our diets. These are the foods – the things, the experiences and the relationships – that you will need to purge, not only from your diet, but first from your pantry. In other words, they need to be put completely off limits *today*.

I will describe each food group and then you will be asked to draw a corresponding picture and to identify "foods" in your cupboard that fit that description.

1. *Unhealthy, dangerous or sinful relationships* – These are relationships that are stolen, manipulative, abusive, or belong on someone else's plate. We discussed co-dependency in Week 2, so you should know by now if you have a relationship that needs to go. While you may have an unhealthy relationship with someone you cannot break away from or even want to break away from (a family member for instance), if you are in an unhealthy relationship you need to get the necessary help to make that relationship wholesome and healthy again. There is absolutely no room in your pantry for unhealthy relationships.

For the sake of cleaning out our pantry, let's picture these relationships as spoiled food such as bread that has passed its expiration date and is now growing moldy.

- Draw a picture of moldy bread below and label it with any relationships you need to get rid of or get help for, using initials only.

2. *Addictive substances* – These are things or substances that are addictive in nature and therefore they keep you in bondage. Look under the Cotton Candy, Stolen Candy, and Deceptive Packaging categories especially for these things, though they can show up anywhere. If you are constantly drawn to any substance in an addictive way, then you need to purge it from you cupboards. It cannot stay. You cannot dabble in it nor have it occasionally. Alcohol, drugs, cigarettes, caffeine, chocolate, powdered sugar donuts all potentially fall into this category if you are in any sort of bondage to them. Don't play games with these. They are dangerous. If you can drink a glass of wine with dinner and don't *need* it (and you know the difference), fine. The purpose of this study is not to arbitrarily label things good or bad. But if you are *pulled* to a substance or you go to it repetitively, then you need to label it correctly and toss it. Let's picture these items as a bottle of alcohol just because that is known to be an addictive substance for many people.

- Draw a picture of a bottle of alcohol and label it with any substances you need to get rid of, once again using initials or code words if you wish.

3. *Consuming habits* – These are activities or experiences that are addictive and consuming. You will know these by the pull they have on you, the amount of time you spend on them, and the money you invest because of them. Review any of the first six food categories to find these activities. They might include, but are not limited to, soap operas, pornography, romance novels, the Internet (Facebook, blogging, chatting, surfing), shopping, etc. Let's

picture these items as a bag of Lay's potato chips because you know what they say about Lay's: You can't eat just one.

- Draw a picture of a bag of chips and label it with any experience or activity you need to get rid of, once again using code words if you wish.

With these three dangerous and even lethal food categories in mind, please read Acts 3:19 in your Bible and write it on a 4x6 index card to be added to your memory album.

Acts 3:19 instructs us to repent of our sins, turn away from them and walk in the other direction, so that two things can occur. First, we will be forgiven and cleansed of our unrighteous behavior. But secondly, we must turn away from our old habits and hang-ups so that a new time of refreshing can begin. When we put away those sinful and often addictive substances, habits, and relationships, God will then begin a re-nourishing process in our lives we've yet to see the likes of. We often have a difficult time letting go of the old and familiar sins because we're afraid they will leave a gaping empty place. They will. But in that empty place, Acts 3:19 assures us, God will pour out His refreshment and it will be so much sweeter and satisfying than anything we have let go of.

Please pen a short prayer repenting of any sinful things you have been going to for filling, thanking God for His forgiveness and asking Him to do His refreshing work in you through His presence.

Six Specific Types of "Food" to Re-label and Keep in Appropriate Quantities

Now for the good news. Hopefully you have some foods left on your soul hunger plates that did not have to be thrown away. While these foods may have truthfully fallen into one of the first six food categories, indicating that you have been consuming them for the wrong reasons or in the wrong quantities or order, they are redeemable. That's right. You don't, fortunately, have to get rid of the children you've been looking to for significance or the friendship you've been going to for companionship. Neither do you have to purge your pantry of your work or most of your hobbies. And while food or even exercise may currently be an addiction for you, you can find a proper place on your shelves for these things, too. You just need to affix new labels to them and learn their appropriate places in your life.

Please read the following descriptions of the six healthy food groups I've identified. You may read as many or as few of the scriptures as you choose. Then draw the corresponding picture and label it accordingly.

1. *Healthy relationships* – Healthy relationships are those in which both parties have proper boundaries in place and they are mutually respected. These are relationships that God has given you and on which you consistently recognize His hand of blessing. They are marked by mutual respect, honor, godliness, proper authority, purity, and holiness. For the purpose of correctly labeling things in our freshly cleaned pantry, we'll picture healthy friendships as spice jars – each one a little different, adding a little something special to our lives. Still, a little spice goes a long way and you would never make a complete meal from a spice!

• Need some help identifying healthy relationships? Read the following scriptures for clarification and take notes as desired: Proverbs 17:17; Proverbs 27:6, 9; Deuteronomy 5:16; Ephesians 6:1, 4; Genesis 2:24; Ecclesiastes 9:9.

• Draw a picture of several spice jars and label them with the names of people you are in healthy relationships with.

2. *Work* – God gives us work to do and He means for us to do it well and gain some degree of satisfaction from it. But once again, work must be assigned the correct label and used for the right purposes. Let's picture work as a stick of butter, for in many ways it butters our daily bread. Most of us need to work in order to have a home to live in and food to put on our table. Our work is a way of cooperating with God to receive His blessings.

- Need some help identifying a healthy helping of work? Read the following scriptures for clarification and take notes as desired: Genesis 2:15; Exodus 34:21; Psalm 62:12; Psalm 90:17; Psalm 127:1-2; 2 Thessalonians 3:10-12.

- Draw a picture of a stick of butter and label it with the types of work you do. As a tool for measuring a healthy serving, designate the average number of hours per week you think would be *healthy* to give to each job.

3. *Nice things* – Having a few nice possessions can certainly make life a little sweeter. That's why we'll picture this category as a jar of jam. But just like a jar of sweet strawberry jam, possessions are meant to be shared with others and indeed taste better when they are. If God has blessed you with nice things, remember to treasure the giver of those gifts above the gift themselves and hold those things with an open palm.

- Need some help identifying a healthy attitude toward nice things? Read the following scriptures for clarification and take notes as desired: Job 1:10; Luke 12:15; 1 Timothy 6:6-10, 17-19.

- Draw a picture of a jar of jam and label it with some of your favorite possessions. Be sure to draw your jar with the lid off and a spoon nearby as a reminder to share those possessions with others.

4. *Good times* – A little pleasure is by no means a sin. In fact, a nice vacation or a little recreation often make days filled with work easier to swallow. God commanded the Israelites to take a Sabbath rest, both weekly and seasonally. Rest, relaxation, and recreation restore us and eventually make us more fit for work and service. So we'll picture the good times as a bottle of cold, refreshing fruit juice. Good times simply need to be balanced with times for work and service. It seems to me that God's idea of balance is somewhere around 6:1, work to rest. So if you're *living* for the good times and find no satisfaction other than when you're on a vacation or at a party, then you might have a problem. One more thing. Even our celebrations and vacations should be Christ-honoring. We may take a vacation from work or household duties, but we don't take a vacation from our walk with the Lord.

- Need some help identifying a healthy attitude toward the good times such as vacations and recreational activities? Read the following scriptures for clarification and take notes as desired: Leviticus 23:23-32; Ecclesiastes 3:1-13.

- Draw a picture of a bottle of juice and label it with some of your favorite good times: vacations, recreational activities, celebrations, etc.

5. *Hobbies* – Even some of our favorite Bible heroes seemingly had hobbies. David played the harp and wrote poetry. From Paul's writings one would suspect that perhaps he favored watching athletic events. And even Jesus seems to have enjoyed an occasional fishing trip. Once again, there's nothing wrong with a wholesome pastime, especially one that puts to good use your gifts or talents. We'll liken our hobbies and pastimes to a jar of honey that simply sweetens the bread on which we are to feast daily. We wouldn't want to make a meal of honey, nor should we try to gain all of our satisfaction from our hobbies.

- Need some help identifying a healthy attitude toward your hobbies and pastimes? Read the following scriptures for clarification and take notes as desired: 1 Samuel 18:10; Proverbs 31:13, 17, 27, 31.

- Draw a picture of a jar of honey and label it with some of your favorite hobbies and pastimes.

6. *Ministry* – A productive and God-ordained ministry is what makes your life salty and appealing to lost people. It is your opportunity to season the world around you with the gospel and the love of God. A ministry can be anything from teaching Bible studies to rocking babies in the church nursery to visiting senior adults who can't get out of their homes to watching a neighbor's child each day until his parents get home from work. Your ministry should be one God has called you to and equipped you for. That is the kind of ministry that will bring the most fulfillment and joy. But even a ministry is just a condiment when we are seeking to have our soul hungers satisfied. Beware of confusing ministry *for God* with a relationship *with God*. Your ministry is not a full meal, but just a salt shaker full of salt, ready to be poured out.

- Need some help identifying a healthy attitude toward your ministry? Read the following scriptures for clarification and take notes as desired: Matthew 5:13; Romans 12:3-8; 1 Corinthians 12:4-7; Galatians 6:2; Ephesians 2:10.

- Draw a picture of a salt shaker and label it with your ministry or ministries.

Dear friend, did you notice that we have now taken out of our pantry anything that is absolutely toxic or harmful to us? We have also relabeled everything else that remains as a condiment or side of sorts. You should only have a variety of spices, a stick of butter (marked with appropriate serving sizes), a jar of jam to share freely, a bottle of fruit juice, honey and salt remaining in your pantry – none of which you should be tempted to make a complete meal from.

As you may have guessed, we have cleaned out our pantry, not so we'll starve our souls, but in order to make room for that which truly satisfies: the Bread of Life.

_ᑘ_

Summary

This week we learned the good news that it's not too late to return to the King's table and eat like a princess, regardless of how many empty cisterns we may have dipped our water jars into in the past. Our first memory verse, Isaiah 55:2 reminds us to quit paying for that which promises to fill but really doesn't, and instead to eat what is good and to delight in His abundance.

We also began looking at a nine-step plan for eating from the Bread of Life. We covered the first three steps:

1. Invite Jesus to work in your life.
2. Evaluate your current diet.
3. Sort out your pantry.

So far we have learned that God can only satisfy our soul desires if Jesus has been invited to move in and take charge in our life. We began learning Philippians 4:19 so that we could remember that God will supply all of our needs through our relationship with Jesus Christ. Apart from that relationship, there are no promises of fulfillment.

We tried to honestly evaluate what we've been "paying money for" that actually doesn't satisfy. We began memorizing Acts 3:19 to remind us not to go back to those "foods" that really don't produce good results in our lives. This scripture also promises us that we can anticipate God doing a refreshing work in our lives through His presence once we have turned away from idols and empty cisterns we have been depending on. We sorted out our pantries, not only by getting rid of some toxic and dangerous "foods", but by changing the labels of some people, things, or experiences so they could stay. Now our pantries should be nicely stocked with a variety of spices, a stick of butter, a jar of jam, a bottle of fruit juice, honey and salt. But, because we can't make a meal of any of these things alone, we're making plenty of room for the Bread of Life.

Week 3
Discussion Questions

1. What are some of the things that really do not satisfy but for which we tend to "spend money," as in Isaiah 55:2? What have we culturally been duped into believing will bring great satisfaction?

2. Why do we struggle so with scripture memory? Have you ever been helped by a memorized scripture? If applicable, share how memorizing scripture has helped you grow spiritually.

3. According to Philippians 4:19, how does God supply all of our needs? Why is this an important scripture to know as we learn how to have our soul hungers satisfied?

4. What does it mean to you to be satisfied? According to the scriptures you looked at on Day 3, how does God satisfy? To what extent and with what quality?

5. Share some of the soul hungers with which you titled your plates on Day 3 and compare them to those listed by the others in your group. What is the difference between a soul hunger and a fleshly desire?

6. According to the food categories listed on Day 4, good things can become bad foods. How is that? What are some of the ways we tend to take what is meant for our good and turn it into an unhealthy food for our souls?

7. What are the three specific types of food that need to be flushed down the drain? Why must we get rid of these completely? What are we supposed to do if a person like a relative falls into this category?

8. Now that you have the appropriate foods labeled correctly as spices, butter, jam, fruit juice, honey, and salt, how hard will it be to keep those foods in their correct portions and to use them wisely so they don't become the main course? Why do you think it was necessary to clean out our pantries?

Week 4 – A New Diet Plan

For some reason ever since Adam and Eve first lived in the Garden of Eden the forbidden and off-limits have tempted our taste buds. Eve had plenty of delicious delicacies to feast on, no doubt. But that forbidden fruit made her mouth water in a way it never had before.

Actually, I'm not so sure a salivating mouth is what drove her to pluck the fruit from the tree of the knowledge of good and evil. Though God could have fulfilled her soul's every desire, I believe it was a gnawing hunger in her soul that the serpent tapped into. In fact, he lied to her and made her doubt the very One who could satisfy her completely. Then he had her turn her attention to an unhealthy and unsatisfactory substitute.

We just spent a long, hard week identifying our usual substitutes. We've identified them for what they are and purged them from our pantry. But we can't leave the pantry empty except for a few select condiments. If we don't fill our souls with something healthy and satisfying, we'll likely return to our old habits in no time flat.

So this week we'll continue to learn how to make a hearty diet of the Bread of Life, how to feast on Him so we'll hunger for no other. It's not just a matter of getting full so we don't gorge on the wrong stuff, though. Sweet sister, Jesus is not just a rice cake you eat so you'll stay away from the temptations on the buffet line. He *is* the buffet!

Day 1
Step 4 – Develop a Refined Palate

I have a blogger friend who just posted this morning that her doctor has requested she begin a new diet due to her recently diagnosed hypoglycemia. She pointed out that she doesn't need to lose weight; she just needs to change her diet to one that is higher in fiber, protein, and vegetables, and zilch on sugar. Out with the bad and in with the good. As my friend posted, this new diet will require quite an adjustment on her part. She'll have to change her tastes, satisfy her hungers with wiser choices, and resist the temptation to revert to the sugary stuff when hunger strikes. But in the long run, she'll be healthier and happier because of the switch.

You and I find ourselves with a similar challenge today. We've identified that which needs to be eliminated and we have cleaned out our soul pantries of that which does not belong. But we're not putting ourselves on a soul starvation diet. We have One who longs to satisfy our every soul hunger. We just need to allow Him to do so.

So the fourth step in learning to feast on the Bread of Life is simply developing a refined palate for Him. We'll look at several scriptures to help us determine how we can refine our tastes so that when we feel the first pangs of soul hunger we are immediately inclined to run to Jesus for satisfaction instead of any other person, thing or experience. We want to crave Him above everything else.

Please read each scripture and fill in the blanks to complete the summary statements. I'm using the New American Standard Bible, but I'm summarizing the scriptures into statements that will help us reflect on their meanings.

Psalm 34:8

_____ and see how good God is! You will find such blessing when you run to Him.

Psalm 119:103

How _____ are the Lord's promises to my _____. They taste sweeter than honey in my mouth!

Dear friend, only God can satisfy your soul hungers and here's the kicker. He does it well! He honors our hunger with true and lasting satisfaction. And what He offers is not just good *for* you; it's plain out *good*. It smells wonderful, tastes delightful, goes down smoothly, and sits well with you. But most of us, even though we may have known God for years, have not really learned to appreciate the quality of that which He offers. Our palates need to be refined. That's why David invites us in Psalm 34:8 to taste and see just how good God is. And in Psalm 119:103 he assures us that His life-giving words are sweeter than honey to the palate.

Please read Psalm 63:1-5 and mark the following words and their synonyms and pronouns in distinctive ways or with colored pencils.

- **God**
- **seek, yearn, thirst**
- **soul**
- **satisfied**

1. According to verse 1, what is David's predicament? What is the condition of his soul?

2. According to the same verse, what does he plan to do about it? When and how?

3. In verses 2 and 3 we find out why David is pursuing God when his soul is thirsty. List what all David says about God in these verses.

4. How satisfied is David when he seeks filling from the Lord, according to verses 4-5? What is his reaction?

David had developed a refined palate. He knew who could really satisfy his soul. How did he know? David was in the wilderness of Judah when he wrote this psalm. He was at a place where no one and nothing else could satisfy. He had been driven to depend only on the Lord to meet the longings of his soul.

Please read 1 Samuel 22:1-5 and 1 Samuel 23:14. This time period is possibly when David penned Psalm 63. Describe David's circumstances during this time.

Did you notice in Psalm 63 that David specifically said his soul was thirsty *for God*? That even his flesh was yearning and fainting *for God*? If I were in David's predicament I might have interpreted the thirsts of my soul as longing for physical help, comfort, relief from the stress, or a rescue of some sort. I might have expected my family, the king of Moab, the prophet Gad, or the men who had gathered around to meet my needs. But David had developed a discerning palate. He seemed to know that nothing could quench his soul thirst like God could.

And that is our goal today. We need to recognize that God can indeed satisfy our every need with good things. He needs to become the one we consistently go to when we are hungry for anything and everything our souls could possibly desire.

Please read over my suggestions for refining our palates and the accompanying scriptures. Make notes as you wish. These suggestions are based on the practices and petitions of David.

- *Ask God to increase your hunger for Him.* Ask Him to give you a craving for His Word, His truths, and His promises. Psalm 119:36-38

- *Ask God each morning to satisfy whatever your soul may hunger for that day.* Tell Him you will be eagerly anticipating Him meeting your needs and that you trust Him to do so. Psalm 90:14, Psalm 138:3, Psalm 143:8

- *Intentionally leave room for God to satisfy your hungers.* Resist the temptation to run elsewhere, and wait on Him instead. Don't be afraid of the empty spaces or the hunger pangs. Psalm 37:7-8, Psalm 43:5

- *Consistently eat healthily and your palate will adjust to the finer things with time.* The more you feast on the Word of God, the more it will delight you. The more you worship the God of the Word, the more you will love and seek Him out. Psalm 25:4-6, Psalm 94:19

- *Get to know Jesus.* When the people said in John 6:34, "Lord, evermore give us this bread," Jesus responded by revealing to them *who He was.* He said, "I am the Bread of Life." (John 6:35) When the woman at the well asked for the living water Jesus had spoken of, He did the same thing. "I who speak to you am He (the Messiah)." (John 4:26) The better you know Jesus, the more you will hunger and thirst for Him. Want to get to know Him? Read through the Gospels.

Please record Psalm 107:8-9 on a 4x6 index card for your memory album. In the top right corner label the card, "God Satisfies with Good."

Recently when my son was home from college I prepared one of his favorite dishes, chicken parmesan. Since he's home so rarely and he doesn't get a good home-cooked meal very often, I wanted to make it just to his liking. When it came time to assemble the pasta, the chicken topped with cheese, and the marinara sauce on the plates, I couldn't remember how Daniel liked his. Did he want the pasta and sauce to the side of the chicken? Did he want the sauce under the chicken or over the chicken? He's pretty picky about what's touching what, you know. I wanted to get it right, so I asked him. His response? "I'm not that picky anymore, Mom. Just fix it how you want to."

After I shut my gaping mouth I turned to the stove, picked up a plate and prepared his meal the same way I did everyone else's. My boy has grown up and his palate has been refined (just a little) in the process. I'd been told my kids' tastes would develop with time and I guess it's true.

Undoubtedly, the longer you and I walk with the Lord, the more mature our palates will become too. Over time we would naturally begin to long for Him above other things. People would disappoint, things would not satisfy like we thought they would, and experiences would leave us lacking, so we'd gradually turn more and more to God for fulfillment.

But I don't want to wait for time to develop my taste for the God who satisfies like no other. I don't have that kind of precious time to waste on trying to satisfy my soul with a lot of foolish stuff.

I want, today, to have a persistent hankering for my God. I desire to taste and see that indeed He is good, so good that nothing else will do.

Let's end our time today praying for God to develop within us a driving hunger and a persistent thirst for Him and Him alone. Let's commit to pouring out our soul needs to Him every morning and expectantly waiting for Him to satisfy those needs. And finally, let's promise to spend more time digesting the sweetness of His Word and getting to know His Son so that our palates are ready for the good stuff.

I invite you to write your prayer in the space below.

Day 2
Step 5 — Identify Your Hungers Correctly

Have you ever eaten a handful of M&Ms because you were disappointed in something or someone? Have you ever plopped down in front of the television because you were bored? Have you ever gone for a run or a walk because you were angry? Or maybe you've burst into tears because you were misunderstood and frustrated.

Remember when we talked about coping mechanisms? If you've ever eaten out of depression, gone for a walk because you're angry or poured yourself a glass of wine because you're lonely, you've tried to cope with a specific soul hunger by satisfying it with a substitute, a coping mechanism. Some of those substitutes are lousy and dangerous. Others aren't bad for you (e.g., going for a walk), but unless you go on to identify the real need and have it met, the emptiness will just continue.

All of us occasionally misdiagnose our needs, whether they are the deep soul issues or just physical needs. We assume we need one thing when indeed the greater need lies elsewhere. For instance, I sometimes mistake my need for rest with a need to eat. I feel myself drooping, running out of steam. What do I do? I often head into the kitchen and scan the refrigerator for something to give me a boost. But often my real need is a break from my work, a twenty-minute power nap, or some recreational release like a walk around the block. Because I haven't diagnosed my need correctly, I attempt to satisfy it incorrectly. Thus the need lingers even after I've had a snack.

What spiritual, emotional or physical needs do you sometimes misdiagnose and how do you mistakenly try to satisfy them?

When the need or hunger is one of a spiritual or emotional nature, the stakes are higher. If I misdiagnose my need for sleep as a desire for something chocolate, I may take in too many calories and not get the sleep I really need. But if I attempt to fill my need for companionship with anything in a bottle, I'm actually opening a door for Satan, the great counterfeiter, to do a number on me. Every soul need I have presents an opportunity for God to pour out His gracious abundance to me. He wants to satisfy those genuine soul needs with good things. But every misdiagnosed soul hunger presents an opportunity for Satan, the enemy, to sneak in a lousy substitute and then taunt me with claims that God doesn't care or doesn't know how to provide for me. Why? Because the substitute fails to satisfy and I'm left wondering why I'm not living the abundant life God promised.

Below I've listed a few genuine soul hungers. Beside each one, list how you sometimes misdiagnose the legitimate desires. I'll get you started with some of my own, but feel free to add to mine.

Soul Hunger	I sometimes misdiagnose this hunger as needing ....
Significance	*attention, accomplishment, success, invitations ...*
Love	*my way, attention, gifts...*
Companionship	*food...*
Refreshment	

If my soul is really hungry for significance, the feeling that I matter, but I interpret those hunger pangs as a need for attention from people, I can easily get frustrated. I begin to think that what I really need is for people to notice me, include me, and fawn over me. When they don't, or I don't perceive they're doing it enough, then I get angry. Not only do I get angry with people and develop resentments toward them, but I become angry with God because He's not meeting my need. Problem is He wants to. He wants to meet the need for significance, a very legitimate need. But He's not obligated to cause people to clamor over me.

On the other hand, if I recognize I have a hunger to feel significant and I identify that need correctly, I can take it to God and He will very easily and graciously address that need. How? Where? Through His Word. He speaks truth into my need, I believe it (take Him at His Word), and the satisfying process begins. Even if God uses a word of encouragement from a friend to meet my need for significance, encouragement will probably come in the form of her speaking truth into my life. That's how God works. Remember Hebrews 4:12 tells us God's Word is alive and has the supernatural ability to penetrate our souls.

Just for practice, let's see what God has to say about your desire for *significance*. How does He meet this need through His Word? Read the following scriptures and summarize what they say about your significance to God.

Psalm 118:7 –

Psalm 139:17-18 –

Ephesians 2:4 –

Colossians 3:12 –

John 3:16 –

When I correctly identify that for which my soul is hungering, I can take that need to God with great anticipation that He will satisfy it completely. But when I misdiagnose my needs, I don't even look to God to meet my needs because I assume I need something He can't provide. I then expect other people, things, or experiences to meet those needs.

Read the following scriptures and summarize what the psalmist has identified his need to be in each.

Psalm 41:4 –

Psalm 55:4-5 –

Psalm 57:1-3 –

Psalm 109:21-26 –

But what's a gal to do when she honestly can't figure out what it is she needs? Haven't we all had times when we knew we needed something, but we couldn't put a finger on it? Those can be frustrating times. And don't you know Satan just sits around waiting for those prime opportunities to move in and frustrate us even more?

What happens when you feel like you're lacking something, but you just don't know what it is? When you have that longing for some unidentifiable something how do you *usually* respond?

Read Psalm 139:23 with the previous question in mind. How do you think David would instruct us when we know our soul yearns for something but we just can't quite identify it?

You may have noticed from reading the Psalms that David was not always on target when he expressed his needs to the Lord. Sometimes he overshot, to put it nicely. He expressed to God that he "needed" Him to wipe out his enemies, to destroy them in wrath, and to shame those who caused him pain. But David's raw, emotional plea did not repulse or surprise God. In the same way, we can express our gut level desires and wishes to God. In fact that is the healthiest thing to do with even our most unhealthy desires. Once we express them to God, He can redirect our hearts by speaking truth to our situations.

As we draw today's lesson to a close, I encourage you to spend a little more time thinking about what it is your soul is craving when you begin to feel those hunger pangs in your spirit. Ask yourself, "What is it my soul is hungry for? What am I really craving deep within?" Take your need to God and allow Him to speak His truth to your need. But if you can't identify the needs of your soul, just tell that to God too. As David wrote in Psalm 139, He knows you inside and out. He created you just the way you are with your unique set of needs and desires. And even in this moment of discontent He can search you through and through and know what your anxious thoughts are all about. He is not offended by your needs and He does not grow weary of tending to them. He loves for you to tell Him what you need and then wait for Him to satisfy you.

May the words of Psalm 38:9 be true of us as they consistently were of David.

"Lord, all my desire is before Thee;
and my sighing is not hidden from Thee."

Please record Psalm 38:9 on a 4x6 index card and add it to your album for meditation and memorization. Label the card "Making My Needs Known."

om

Day 3
Step 6 — Prepare Ahead a Satisfying Menu

A couple of years ago as my husband and I began to seriously consider how we would afford to send our son to college, I began to fret and be anxious. I desperately needed encouragement and affirmation for the future. Though I was praying for God to provide and knew He would, my fears were getting the best of me.

While I knew the truth, that God would provide and work all of these things out for our good, my soul needed to be reassured, calmed, and encouraged. Other people would tell me their stories of

God's faithfulness and that helped some, but their situations were different from mine and they could give me no guarantees. People were not able to satisfy my soul's hunger for reassurance.

Finally I took my need to God. I told Him not only that I needed for Him to provide financially for my son's college, but I needed Him to give me assurance and peace in the interim as I waited for His plan to unfold. After I expressed my need to Him, I searched for scriptures that spoke to my soul hunger. I found truths in His Word that would encourage my heart and calm my fears. I discovered words of hope and peace and truth to feast on in my times of deep soul hunger.

That's the next step in learning to feast continually on the Bread of Life so that we experience lives of abundant satisfaction instead of desperation. Through soul-searching and prayer, we need to determine what it is we long for and then go to God's Word to prepare a feast of truth with which to feed our hungry souls.

Either look back at your assignment on Week 3, Day 3 and identify two of your most pressing soul hungers or simply determine afresh what your soul has craved lately. Name two of your soul hungers:

_____   _____

I know it's not always easy to determine what your soul is hungry for. This can be some deep stuff! But don't try to make it harder than necessary. In different seasons of life you may hunger:

- to feel significant, important, to matter
- to experience unconditional love and acceptance
- for forgiveness, a clean conscience, grace
- for purpose, a calling, meaning, direction
- to have companionship, friendship, conversation
- to experience adventure, variety, new horizons
- for encouragement, strength, fortification, stamina, courage
- for energy, refreshment, renewal, vitality
- to experience family, intimacy, closeness with another

If you're not especially "hungry" right now, just choose one of the soul hungers I mentioned in the bulleted list. My bet is you'll be hungry for at least one of these things in the near future. And if you named a soul hunger that's not on the list, that's ok too.

Today we learn how to build an ample and satisfying menu of truth from which to feast when our souls are hungry. Why do we need to have scriptures already in hand to feed our hungers? Why aren't we just praying for God to meet our needs and leaving it at that? Because God feeds us and satisfies our hungers *through His Word.*

Please read the following scriptures, marking these words and their synonyms:

- **fed, feed, eat, eats**
- **manna**
- **bread**
- **Word (what "proceeds out of the mouth of the Lord"?)**
- **truth**

- **Jesus (I)**
- **live, lives**
- **flesh**

"And He humbled you and let you be hungry, and fed you with manna which you did not know, nor did your fathers know, that He might make you understand that man does not live by bread alone, but manlives by everything that proceeds out of the mouth of the Lord." *Deuteronomy 8:3 (NASB)*

In the beginning was the Word, and the Word was with God, and the Word was God....And the Word became flesh and dwelt among us, and we beheld His glory, glory as of the only begotten from the Father, full of grace and truth. *John 1:1, 14 (NASB)*

"I am the bread of life. Your fathers ate the manna in the wilderness, and they died. This is the bread which comes down out of heaven, so that one may eat of it and not die. I am the living bread that came down out of heaven; if anyone eats of this bread, he shall live forever; and the bread also which I shall give for the life of the world is My flesh." *John 6:48-51 (NASB)**
*Note: The context of this scripture is the conversation Jesus had with the crowd who followed Him after He had amply satisfied their hunger with the bread and fish.

List what you learned about the Word or that which "proceeds out of the mouth of the Lord."

List what you learned about Jesus.

Sweet sister, did you see that God has said we live by that which proceeds out of His mouth, which of course would be His Word? Did you notice that Jesus, God's only begotten Son, *is* the Word of God? And did you notice that Jesus referenced the Father's statement in Deuteronomy 8:3 when He said in John 6 that *He* is the bread of life sent from heaven? Finally, did you see that Jesus said we must *eat* Him?

I have a difficult time wrapping my brain around all of that. In fact, I honestly do not completely understand how Jesus and the Word of God can be one and the same. But that is what the scripture says and so I choose to believe it.

Please complete the following "equation" using the truths you learned from our three scriptures. You'll have to figure out the answer by adding the truths together.

Jesus is the _____ of life. (John 6:48)
+
Jesus said we must _____ His flesh to live. (John 6:51)
+
Jesus is also the _____ who became flesh. (John 1:14)
+
Man lives by that which proceeds from the _____ of God. (Deuteronomy 8:3)
=
To live we must _____ God's Word.

Please read one more scripture and consider it in light of what we've already read and learned.

For as many as may be the promises of God, in Him they are yes; wherefore also by Him is our Amen to the glory of God through us. *2 Corinthians 1:20 (NASB)*

From 2 Corinthians 1:20 we learn that apart from a relationship with Jesus the Word of God does not necessarily satisfy us, but in a relationship with Christ Jesus God's Word is "yes" to us. In fact, I would bet that a lost person finds God's Word to be very *dis*satisfying.

When we feast on the truths of *God's Word*, the Bible, within a thriving relationship with *God's Word*, Jesus, we find complete satisfaction for our souls. We live and we live abundantly. That, dear friend, is where it's at!

Today I will provide some scriptures that truthfully address a handful of soul hungers. However, you must be equipped to find scriptures that address the desires of *your* soul. Sweet sister, this is not hard. It just requires a teachable heart, anticipation for God to speak, and a little effort on your part. Here's how you can find applicable and practical truths to feed your every soul desire.

- **Expose yourself to God's truth *systematically* and *consistently*.** Enroll in a Bible study, read the Bible through, use a daily devotional guide, attend a Bible-teaching church weekly and/or listen to biblically sound messages via radio or podcasts. I don't recommend the "open your Bible and see where it lands" method. God's Word deserves more respect than that.

- **Earnestly ask God to give you scriptures that speak to your soul hunger.** Pay attention to scriptures used in your Bible study class, your pastor's sermon, a daily devotional or anywhere else you see or hear scripture used responsibly. See if God doesn't provide truths that speak specifically to your needs in due time.

- **Ask for help.** Ask friends, a Bible study teacher, your pastor, or a mentor for help locating scriptures that speak to your particular need.

- **Use a Bible promise book or a reputable Christian book that addresses your need to find appropriate scriptures.**

- **Use the simple concordance found in the back of most Bibles or a larger exhaustive concordance.** Simply choose a key word that pertains to that hunger and look it up in the concordance. The concordance will list scriptures containing that word. While not all of those verses will actually speak to your hunger, some will.

I cannot stress enough the value of writing down applicable scriptures, keeping them in an album, and meditating on them each day. I know teachers like Beth Moore and others have been encouraging this method of feeding your soul for years, but so few women take advantage of this tool. That's a shame because it really does work. So I'm begging you, if you haven't already done so get your album and index cards today and join us in writing these scriptures down and meditating on them regularly. If you memorize them, great. But meditating on them daily is the real key.

Choose at least four scriptures that speak to one of your soul needs and write them on 4x6 index cards for your memory album. You may use the ones listed here and/or find others.

Significance
Psalm 118:7
Psalm 139:17-18
Ephesians 2:4
Colossians 3:12
John 3:16

Love
Jeremiah 31:3
John 15:9
John 15:13
1 John 3:1
Romans 5:8
Romans 8:37-39
Ephesians 3:19

Companionship
Exodus 33:11a
Deuteronomy 31:8
Psalm 23:4
Psalm 27:4-6
Psalm 55:17
Isaiah 43:1-2
John 15:14-15

Purpose
Isaiah 43:18-19
Jeremiah 29:11
Psalm 90:17
Psalm 66:16
Matthew 28:19-20
Romans 12:1-2

Rest, Refreshment
Matthew 11:28-30
Psalm 37:7
Isaiah 40:28-31
Jeremiah 31:25
Acts 3:19
Psalm 32:3-5

Strength, Courage
Joshua 1:9
Psalm 118:6
Psalm 94:17-19
Psalm 91:11-12
Psalm 27:14
John 16:33
2 Corinthians 4:17-18

One last scripture. Please write Deuteronomy 8:3 on a 4x6 index card and add it to your album. You can label it "Eating the Word of God."

God's Word contains every truth you need in order to live a content life. It is our daily bread and by it we can be satisfied completely in Christ Jesus. But don't wait until you are ravenous and cranky before you stock your pantry with its truth. Begin today to select and meditate on at least a handful of biblical truths so that you can live an abundantly satisfied life.

M

Day 4
Step 7 – Go to God Daily and First

Before we go any further let's review the first six steps of this eight step plan for feasting on the Bread of Life. Flip through the last couple of weeks of this study if you need to in order to complete the following chart. I've put the steps in the titles of most lessons.

Step 1 Invite _____ **to work in your life.**

Step 2 _____ **your current diet.**

Step 3 _____ _____ **your pantry.**

Step 4 Develop a _____ **palate.**

Step 5 Identify your _____ _____.

Step 6 Prepare _____ **a satisfying menu.**

Now that you've prepared a menu of soul satisfying truths from God's Word, you have immediate access when those hunger pangs start. But long before we reach the point of starvation, it is a wise decision to have a steady diet of truth. When you feast continuously on the daily bread of the Bible and allow Jesus, the Bread of Life, to apply it to your soul, you will experience fewer and fewer moments of ridiculously ravenous hunger.

Please read Psalm 107:4-9 in your Bible. Answer the following questions:

1. Which verse indicates *when* they cried out to the Lord in their hunger?

2. What did they do *before* they cried out to him?

3. What was the condition of their soul by the time they cried out to God?

4. Even though they waited so long before crying out to God, what was the result?

Please read the following scriptures and underline the phrases that indicate the answer to the questions "When?" and/or "How often?"

Psalm 5:3
In the morning, O Lord, Thou wilt hear my voice; in the morning I will order my prayer to Thee and eagerly watch.

Psalm 1:2-3
But his delight is in the law of the Lord, and in His law he meditates day and night. And he will be like a tree firmly planted by streams of water, which yields its fruit in its season, and its leaf does not wither; and in whatever he does, he prospers.

Psalm 68:19
Blessed be the Lord, who daily bears our burden, the God who is our salvation.

Psalm 88:1
O Lord, the God of my salvation, I have cried out by day and in the night before Thee.

Psalm 90:14
O satisfy us in the morning with Thy lovingkindness, that we may sing for joy and be glad all our days.

According to these scriptures and the psalmists' habits, when and how often do you think you need to take your soul desires to God and meditate on His truths?

What is your plan for taking your soul needs to God each day and eating a steady diet of the Bread of Life? This is important; be specific.

I gave you the opportunity to answer that last question before I provided my own answer because I think it's important that you come up with a plan that will work for you. When it comes to physically eating, some people like me prefer to eat three square meals a day beginning with breakfast and ending with dinner. Other people, like my husband, would rather eat mini meals throughout the day every two hours or so. Still others eat three small meals and a couple of snacks. All three diet plans can produce satisfying results. That's the same kind of plan we need for nourishing our souls, but the options are endless.

Here's how I get a steady diet of the Bread of Life that keeps me satisfied and on track:

- I have a quiet time each morning when I invite Jesus to work in my life, tell Him how I'm feeling about things and what my soul desires, and ask Him to feed me as He sees fit.
- I then feast on a steady diet of the daily bread by reading that day's portion of my *Everyday with Jesus Bible,* a one-year reading Bible.
- I've also put together an album like the one we've been working on that is full of scriptures that speak to my current needs. I read through these scriptures most every morning, meditating on them and applying them to my needs. Sometimes I turn them into prayers and ask God to make those truths "yes in Christ Jesus" in my life.

- Throughout the day, as I have the chance or need, I read through the scriptures again or recite them if they are memorized.
- I participate in a weekly Bible study like this one that requires spending time daily in God's Word.
- I attend my church's worship services and take notes when my pastor preaches. I don't always keep the notes, but if I hear a scripture that speaks to a current need (you got it) I write it down and add it to my album.

My plan keeps me in God's Word on a consistent basis and in a systematic format. I don't just run to the Bible in my moments of desperation, flip it open, close my eyes, and point my finger at some random verse and claim it. Why not? Because if I wait until my soul is desperately starving and then run to the Bible I am more likely to apply its truths irresponsibly and inaccurately. Scarfing down the first scripture my desperate finger lands on may not produce a tummy ache or indigestion, but it also won't result in healthy nourishment for my soul.

One more thing. I want you to know that I don't solely focus on satisfying *my* needs during my daily quiet time, my scripture memory, or my Bible studies. That would be a little piggish, huh? I allow God to convict me, challenge me, open my eyes to the needs of others and instruct me too. I just wanted you to see how each of these spiritual disciplines contribute to my overall feeling of satisfaction, which is, of course, the focus of this Bible study.

Please read Psalm 86:1-7 in your Bible. According to verse 7, when is David calling upon God?

There will be times when our soul hungers attack us out of the blue, when we suddenly need God to "preserve our souls," as David says in verse 2. And in those moments, not only is it ok to run to God in desperation, it is *necessary*. And He desires to be the very first one to whom we turn.

Beware, however. Those moments of desperation will be the precise ones that will tempt you to run right back to the people, things, or experiences you have previously tossed from your pantry or relabeled with healthy, appropriate labels.

When your soul is suddenly hungry with a new desire, where do you think you will be most likely to turn for satisfaction?

Obviously the answer to that question may depend on the type of hunger you are facing, but we need to be vigilantly aware of our tendencies to return to the broken cisterns we have abandoned. Sweet sister, face your habits head on, confess them to God, and ask Him to help you run consistently to the Bread of Life instead of returning to that which will not satisfy.

Continue reading Psalm 86 to its end. Then answer today's final two questions.

1. According to verses 8–10, do you think David bothered to turn anywhere else when his sudden soul hunger hit?

2. Even in this moment of desperation how does David expect God to satisfy his soul? Check all that apply.
   - ☐ through a possible miracle
   - ☐ through His truth
   - ☐ with lovingkindness
   - ☐ halfway
   - ☐ with mercy
   - ☐ graciously
   - ☐ angrily
   - ☐ with abundance
   - ☐ with His strength
   - ☐ possibly through a sign
   - ☐ with help
   - ☐ with comfort
   - ☐ later

Wow! Even in a desperate moment God is definitely the one to run to. He can satisfy like no other. Run to Him...daily and first.

✦

Day 5
Step 8 – Share Dessert with Others

Today at my MOPS (Mothers of Preschoolers) meeting, one of my fellow Mentor Moms shared a word of testimony as a devotional. I could tell she was about to burst to tell her story of something God had done for her. She had already given Him praise in the leadership team's brief prayer meeting before the program began. But now she seemed anxious to verbally give God credit for doing something specific in her life.

The Mentor Mom shared how God had kept her safe recently when someone evidently shot at her while she was driving down the road. That's right; someone had shot an air pistol of some sort at her from directly behind her car as she was driving down the road. Her rear window was shattered, but she was unharmed. She doesn't know exactly how it happened or why, but she knows God met her need for safety. And she didn't merely praise God for keeping her safe, but she told the group how thankful she was to God for assuring her of His love, for making her feel protected and cared for, and for keeping His eye on her.

As I listened to my friend share her story I wondered why she felt so compelled to not only tell the horrific account, but to adamantly give God credit. I've heard other people tell nail-biting stories like this one and never give God any credit even though it was certainly due Him. My friend spent more time singing God's praises than she did elaborating on the scary event. I have a feeling we were not the first group she had touted God's praises to since the incident. As I watched her fight back tears and shake with overwhelming emotion, I began to understand why she needed to praise the Lord. Perhaps when you have truly perceived that God has satisfied a need as only He can do, you really can't help but share your story. You can't help but tell others of the miraculous and hugely satisfying way God has met that need.

This Mentor Mom is a woman who travels a great deal with her business and much of that travel is solo. She undoubtedly has asked God many times to provide safety for her. When His provision came through for her, she didn't ascribe to good luck or fortunate timing or good karma. She knew God had satisfied her need for safety and, without hesitation, she gave Him credit.

What does the psalmist in Psalm 66:16 long to do after God has met his need? Underline the portion of the scripture (provided below) that answers that question.

Come and hear, all who fear God, and I will tell of what He has done for my soul. (Psalm 66:16)

Read Psalm 66:16-20 in your Bible to find out exactly what the psalmist wanted his fellow God followers to know. List your findings in the space below.

Have you ever heard people attributing certain provisions, activity, or good things to God and wondered why they're giving Him credit for something that could have just been a coincidence? More than likely the reason they're giving Him credit is because *He* is the one they went to with the need to begin with.

Once you get into the habit of asking God to meet your soul needs, you'll become more aware of the many ways He answers your requests. You won't take the day's blessings, even the smallest ones, for granted. Not only will you not take things for granted, you'll be more prone to praise the God who *gave* you the blessings as opposed to the blessings themselves. In other words, it may delight you to get a call from a faraway friend and you may enjoy the visit, but you'll recognize that your good God is the one who prompted that call in response to your request for a little companionship. You'll thank the friend for calling, but you'll thank your God for satisfying your soul with a good thing.

Have you experienced any recent blessings, any fulfilled desires that you now recognize as God's satisfying provisions for your soul hungers? Describe one or two and give God the credit and a little gratitude.

The psalmist in Psalm 66 didn't just praise and thank God directly for satisfying the cry of his soul, but he went the extra step of singing God's praises to others. I'm sure, from the things he writes, that He did thank God for meeting his need, but he didn't stop there. His joyful satisfaction compelled him to share God's goodness with anyone who would listen. That's what happens when you learn to take all of your needs to God, not just the usual "prayer requests". Do you understand what I'm talking about?

Unless I'm intentional about taking my *soul needs* to God, I easily slip into what seems to be a universal habit of simply asking God for things like safety, good health, help with a dilemma, financial provision, etc. I make God aware of my situations and I ask Him to help me with those tangible sorts of things, but I don't bother Him with my deeper needs. However, when I deliberately take the time to address the more intimate hungers of my soul and ask God to meet those needs, then wow! He shows

Himself to be intuitive, discerning, compassionate, and intimately acquainted with the cries of my soul. That's when I realize that He truly can satisfy my every need. That's when I fall more deeply in love with my God. And that's when I can't keep quiet about His faithful attention to every detail of my life.

In Psalm 66:16 the psalmist particularly wants to tell others about the work God has done where? (Check the correct answer.)
- □ **on the battlefield**
- □ **at his home**
- □ **in his soul**
- □ **in his bank account**
- □ **in his body**

For some reason we are much more apt to tell other people about physical provisions from God than we are to share "what He has done for my soul." But I've found that when I do tell others how God has blessed my soul, not just my bank account or my physical body, they definitely listen. I certainly want people to know that my God can handle things like helping me raise my kids, saving my marriage, providing for us financially, and giving me a new job. But I also believe people really need to know that my God can strengthen me for foreboding tasks, comfort me in times of grief, provide companionship when I am lonely, give me significance and purpose when I'm floundering, and make me feel beautiful when I just need a lift. He is a practical God, but He is also the lover of my soul.

How has God satisfied your soul recently? How has he met a very personal soul desire for you?

What do you think would be some of the benefits of sharing with others God's goodness to you?

Have you shared with anyone recently what God has done for your soul? When and how?

If not, could you make plans to do that soon? I encourage you to share a satisfied soul need with someone this week. If you're willing, write your plan here.

Add Psalm 66:16 to your memory album so you'll be reminded to tell others what God has done for your soul.

I love going out to eat at a nice restaurant with friends. Usually the conversation is lively, the atmosphere is celebratory, the food is great, and the experience is altogether satisfying for everyone included. Even though we all eat more than we should during those times, it's still fun to order dessert. Most of the time I couldn't possibly eat an entire gooey, chocolate dessert by myself, but I can always go for a little something sweet after the main course. Still, if I were by myself I probably wouldn't order dessert, but since I'm with friends or family I'm game if they are. So what do we inevitably do? You got it. We order one or two desserts, depending on the number at our table, and get enough spoons or forks to go around. We put the sweet thing in the middle of the table and we all dig in with gusto. Dessert just tastes even better when it's shared with others.

If God's satisfying answer to your soul's hunger is like a richly satisfying meal to your belly, then what you do after that hunger has been satisfied is similar to the choice you have after eating your entrée among friends. You can put your fork down, push away from the table and leave satisfied and full. No problem with that option, but the party ends there. But if you'd like to celebrate a little longer, which is always fun, I have a better option for you. Why not feast on God's delicacies a little longer by splitting dessert with others? You can put that sweet and satisfying answer to prayer right in the center of the table and share it with everyone around you. You can point to the delightful thing and say, "Let me tell you what God has done for my soul." Then you can pass out the spoons so everyone can take a bite and you can all praise God's goodness together. God's sweet and satisfying provisions taste even better and last even longer when we share them with others. And don't worry. There's plenty to go around.

৵

Summary

So now we've covered all eight of the steps derived from scripture that help us feast on the Bread of Life.

Step 1   Invite _____ to work in your life.

Step 2   _____ your current diet.

Step 3   _____ _____ your pantry.

Step 4   Develop a _____ palate.

Step 5   Identify your _____ _____ .

Step 6   Prepare _____ a satisfying menu.

Step 7   Go to God _____ and _____ .

Step 8   _____ dessert with others.

Week 4

Discussion Questions

1. Have you ever changed your physical diet, what or how you eat? If so, how did you go about changing your eating habits so that you learned to enjoy healthier foods? Relate your efforts to the process of refining our spiritual palates so that we crave the good things of God.

2. Discuss with your group what hungers, whether spiritual, physical or emotional, you are prone to misdiagnose. Why do you misdiagnose those so often?

3. Is it hard to express your soul needs to God? Why or why not?

4. Using the equation we worked on day three, explain to each other how we go about eating the Bread of Life. Be sure to include why it's important to have a relationship with Jesus Christ.

5. On day three we selected scriptures that speak to one or more of our soul needs with which to prepare ahead a satisfying menu of truth. Share some of your scriptures with your group and explain how God can use those truths to satisfy your soul hungers. If you did not record any scriptures, let you group help you find some that speak to your current need.

6. Share your plan for taking your soul needs to God each day. When, where, and how will you do this?

7. What part does consistent and systematic exposure to God's Word play in having one's soul needs met? Why is this important? How do you accomplish this?

8. How has God satisfied your soul recently? Prepare to share with your group God's provision for your soul need just like you would a rich and decadent dessert. How does sharing of this sort make you feel?

Week 5 – I'm Learning to Be Content

Dear friend, I want you to know that when I first began writing this study I was passionate about the topic, about women learning how they could find complete satisfaction in Christ alone. Passion carried me through the first weeks of writing. As I wrote this study and dwelt on the scriptures and the principles I was writing about, I began to feel fuller than ever. God was showing me that my words were not shallow promises, but based on deep and abiding truth.

During the first several months of writing I felt so complete, so satisfied, and so amazingly content. The principles I felt led to write about were proving to be true in my life like never before. I felt saturated in God's love, like I was the center of His attention, completely at rest in His provisions. I knew without a doubt that the Holy Spirit was fulfilling Jesus' promise in John 16:13 and guiding me into all truth. I felt completely confident passing those truths on to you.

But during the past couple of weeks, as I've written the previous chapter, I have felt the snarly attack of the enemy. I have awakened most every day feeling like I had insufficient funds in my soul. I have lacked purpose, felt lonely, experienced discouragement, and ached for reassurance. I'd like to tell you I immediately put the very principles I've been writing about into practice, but that's not the case. Just like you, I know more truth than I habitually apply to my own life. And, maybe unlike you, I often require the whack of a spiritual two by four on my head before it dawns on me to do the very things I know to do.

Eventually I did begin to practice what I preach. And today, as I begin to put on paper our final lessons, I can say with full confidence, "I've learned *again* to be content." Learning to be content with the soul satisfying goodness of Jesus Christ, our Bread of Life, is not a six-week course. It is a lifelong journey. It requires diligent application of biblical principles and walking daily in truth instead of our emotions. It requires discipline and commitment and belief and focus. Are you up to it?

I believe you are. But these next two weeks of study will be devoted to addressing those little things that will inevitably cause you to feel dissatisfied again unless you are aware of and prepared to confront them. Little lies from the enemy, little temptations that still have a not-so-subtle allure and little common mistakes we all make occasionally.

I've offered this confession today because I want you to know that I write these final weeks of study for me as well as for you. Now, at last, we know how to be completely satisfied. But it's up to us to live in the light of those truths. Let's put them into practice.

Day 1
It Doesn't Come Naturally

Raise your hand if you've ever changed your eating habits – perhaps in order to lose weight, have more energy, lower your cholesterol, etc. – and you *immediately* met with success. Anybody? Didn't think so. It takes time to adjust to new eating schedules, new foods, new restrictions, and the cravings that now have to be denied. In fact, it also takes work.

Finding complete soul satisfaction through Jesus also takes time and, yes, work. Let's face it, if Christians were spontaneously and automatically satisfied through their relationships with Jesus Christ at the time of conversion, the world would be a different place. That contentment would fuel harmonious churches, healthy families, cooperative efforts toward evangelization, and much more. We'd all look like the happy, smiley, sharing folks in one of Coca-Cola's commercials where people are passing out soft drinks left and right to anyone they pass on the street. Only we'd be passing out something much more valuable – the love of Christ.

While such ultimate contentment is the goal, I fear few believers ever learn to be so content that their satisfied souls actually begin to make a difference in the way they relate to others. That's a shame. Really it is.

I'd like for you and I to commit to growing in contentment to the point that we are freed up from personal interests and self-absorption in order to effectively share God's love with the world. Because, sweet sister, that's the ultimate goal. We're not seeking satisfaction just so we can lie in green fields and enjoy the clouds as they form pictures in the sky. We're seeking soul satisfaction so we can pass it on!

Please read Philippians 4:11-12 in your Bible and answer the following questions.

1. How does Paul say he came to be content?

2. By Paul's word choice, how much work do you suppose was involved in becoming a contented person? Mark the following charts with an X.

Snap of the fingers	Hard work

Instantaneous	Over time

By osmosis	Practice and Determination

3. How does Paul define contentment? (vs. 12)

4. What are the circumstantial extremes Paul describes?

5. Do these circumstances appear to have more to do with his physical needs and situations or his soul? Why do you answer as you do?

6. Does Paul in any way infer that he changed his circumstances in order to be content? Or does he allude to achieving an inner contentment despite the outward circumstances?

True contentment is an inner state of being that is achieved regardless of the outer circumstances. Happiness, we would say in our English vernacular, is the state of being surrounded by blissful circumstances that make contentment inevitable. But contentment is being able to say, "It is well with my soul despite or regardless of my circumstances." Are the lyrics of the familiar hymn *It is Well with My Soul* running through your mind right now? That would be a great soundtrack for this particular lesson because the author of that song, Horatio Spafford, found himself in the most difficult of circumstances, but still contended that his soul was satisfied.

Spafford and his wife Anna were prominent citizens in Chicago in the late 1800s. Up until 1870 things had indeed gone well for the Spaffords. They were a wealthy, influential family. They were also close friends with the famous and effective evangelist D. L. Moody. But in 1870 they lost their four-year-old son, their only son, to scarlet fever. And in 1871 the family's devastating circumstances multiplied when all of Spafford's extensive real estate holdings along the shores of Lake Michigan were wiped out by the great Chicago Fire.

Concerned about the sadness imposed upon his wife and daughters by their son's death and his financial losses, Spafford planned a trip to Europe for the family. Not only would they vacation there, but the family planned to help support D. L. Moody as he preached the gospel overseas. But Horatio was detained by business just before the family was to set sail. Determined to go through with the trip, he sent Anna and the four girls ahead and planned to join them later.

But nine days after his family set sail, Horatio Spafford received a daunting telegram from his wife in Whales. It read: Saved alone. Their ship, the *Ville de Havre*, had collided with the English vessel the *Loch Earn* and had sunk in just 12 minutes, taking the lives of 226 passengers. Anna had clung to her four daughters but later remembered the terror of her baby being swept from her arms by the force of the rushing water as the ship plunged beneath the surface. She survived only because a dislodged plank from the ship miraculously supported her unconscious body and carried her to safety.

Horatio set sail immediately from New York to join his wife. The couple's fifth daughter Bertha, born after the accident, later reported that during her father's passage the captain of the ship had called him to his deck and told him, "A careful reckoning has been made and I believe we are now passing the place where the *de Havre* was wrecked. The water is three miles deep." Horatio Spafford went back to his cabin and penned the words to the now beloved hymn.

It Is Well with My Soul

When peace, like a river, attendeth my way,
When sorrows like sea billows roll;
Whatever my lot, Thou hast taught me to say,
It is well, it is well with my soul.

Chorus:
It is well with my soul,
It is well, it is well with my soul.

Tho' Satan should buffet,
Tho' trials should come,
Let this blest assurance control,
That Christ has regarded my helpless estate,
And hath shed His own blood for my soul.
My sin – oh, the bliss of this glorious tho't:
My sin not in part, but the whole
Is nailed to the cross and I bear it no more,
Praise the Lord, praise the Lord,
O my soul!

And, Lord, haste the day when the faith shall be sight,
The clouds be rolled back as a scroll,
The trump shall resound and the Lord shall descend,
"Even so," it is well with my soul.

Horatio G. Spafford, 1828-1888

Circle the phrase in Horatio Spafford's hymn that indicates that contentment did not come any more naturally to him than it does to you or me, but that he *learned* how to say "it is well with my soul."

Who did Mr. Spafford say taught him to be content in his soul?

It is not my intent to elevate Spafford's words to the level of Scripture, but we can certainly learn from this hero of the faith and from the heartfelt message he penned. I hope you noticed that he said God had taught him to be content whatever his lot. And why could he be content of soul no matter what? Because Christ had taken his helpless estate into regard and shed His blood for his soul. The contentment of our soul always rests in the hands of Jesus. He alone can satisfy our souls. He alone can make it well with our souls, even when all is not well. And when we realize, as did Spafford, that the greatest need of our soul is salvation, we will be so thankful for the cleansing blood of Jesus that every other desire of the soul will pale in comparison. Our hearts will be so full of gratitude there will be no room for discontent.

But while Jesus is the champion of our souls, Satan is the enemy. Even though Jesus has done all that needs to be done to satisfy your soul forever by dying on the cross and paying the penalty for your sin, Satan does not want you to enjoy the satisfaction Christ's gift brings. He is constantly seeking to make you feel *dis*satisfied, *dis*contented, and like all is not well within.

What are some of the ways you have noticed the enemy trying to make you and others feel discontented? Check as many as you wish.

_____comparison

_____ advertising

_____ the American dream

_____ motivational speakers

_____ the affluence of others

_____ television/Hollywood

_____ Facebook

_____ romance novels

_____ other _____

As you begin to walk in the truths we've discovered through this Bible study, it is very likely you will encounter a fresh attack from the enemy. He does not want you to be content. One of his most effective and oft used tactics is to make you believe that God is holding out on you, that He is not even willing to give you all you "deserve" or need.

Please read Genesis 2:7-17 in your Bible and answer the following questions. Check all answers that apply on each question.

1. According to Genesis 2:9, how was the vegetation in the Garden of Eden described?
   - ☐ pleasing to the sight
   - ☐ mundane
   - ☐ tasteless
   - ☐ sub par
   - ☐ good for eating

2. According to this same scripture, it appears the *fruit* from the tree of the knowledge of good and evil was:
   - ☐ no better than the others
   - ☐ much more desirable
   - ☐ the very best fruit
   - ☐ the worst fruit
   - ☐ distinguishable, but not necessarily any better or worse

3. From the biblical description of the Garden of Eden, it sounds like:
   - ☐ paradise
   - ☐ adequate
   - ☐ the slums
   - ☐ satisfying

4. When God told the man what he could eat from the garden he gave him:
   - ☐ freedom
   - ☐ limitations
   - ☐ hardly anything
   - ☐ abundance
   - ☐ sufficient choices
   - ☐ clear consequences

5. God was _____ about what would happen if the man ate from the tree of the knowledge of good and evil.
   - ☐ vague
   - ☐ ambiguous
   - ☐ clear
   - ☐ precise
   - ☐ ugly
   - ☐ tricky

Now read Genesis 3:1-7. Let's answer a few more questions. You can have multiple right answers once again.

1. From the woman's conversation with the crafty serpent it appears she:
   - ☐ realized how sneaky he was
   - ☐ was prepared for his questions and accusations
   - ☐ had her facts straight
   - ☐ was taken unaware by his deceptive accusations
   - ☐ became more discontented the longer she engaged in the conversation with him

2. What insights could you apply from the above question? Think this through.

3. The serpent convinced the woman to take a second look at the forbidden fruit (vs.4&5) by:
   - ☐ showing her a savvy advertisement
   - ☐ lying to her
   - ☐ making her think God was holding out on her
   - ☐ promising something he couldn't deliver on
   - ☐ making God look like the bad guy
   - ☐ singing a catchy jingle

4. In Genesis 3:6 the woman took another look at the fruit from the tree of the knowledge of good and evil and decided it was: (some are stated and some are definitely inferred)
   - ☐ delightful to look at
   - ☐ good for eating
   - ☐ able to make her wise
   - ☐ free for the taking

- ☐ rightfully hers
- ☐ harmless
- ☐ worth taking
- ☐ not worth it

5. Were her assessments correct?
   - ☐ yes
   - ☐ no
   - ☐ some were, some weren't

Dear friend do you see how Satan played Eve for the fool? He will do the same with you and me if we are not on guard for Satan's tactics. We must be fully equipped with truth from God's Word and feasting on the Bread of Life so not to be caught with hungry, unsatisfied souls in the presence of that sneaky snake.

Contentment with Christ does not come naturally. We must actively learn to be content. Contentment requires feasting on truth, going to God with our needs, asking Him to meet them and trusting Him alone to do so. Meanwhile, we must be on the look-out for the deceptive tactics of the enemy. He's a liar, sweet sister. God is *not* holding out on you. He is good and He knows how to satisfy your soul with only the best.

Two final questions and we'll break for the day.

Satan is a student of people. He studies us and knows our individual weaknesses and hang-ups. Eve was obviously allured by beauty and the serpent played to her tendency. If he has studied you and knows your weaknesses and quirks, and I believe he probably has, what will he be targeting? What are some of the things that trigger discontentedness in you?

How can you be more aware and resistant to those triggers so you don't fall susceptible to them? (For instance, I stay away from mail order catalogs as much as possible.)

Day 2
Isn't My Husband Supposed to Do That?

We were going around the circle sharing how God had recently answered our prayers when Genevieve enthusiastically said she had seen some wonderful changes in her marriage over the past several months.

"My husband and I were having the same arguments over and over," said this young mom of three energetic boys. "Do you all do that too?"

Of course everyone nodded yes. I knew exactly what she meant and you probably do too. Spouses tend to see the same shortcomings in each other, have the same unmet needs, and complain about similar problems over and over.

Genevieve looked around the table at the other women and smiled excitedly. She continued, "Then someone told me that instead of taking my issues with my husband to him every time that I should just take them straight to God. I should just tell God what I needed from my husband and let Him do the work. It's made a world of difference. I've begun to see huge changes in how my husband relates to me and just general changes in him, and I haven't had to talk with him about any of it. God has just worked!"

Genevieve has come across one of the most powerful components of a healthy marriage and one of the keys for learning to be content that I wanted to share with you this week.

Many a marriage has taken a detour for the worst because one spouse or both are too demanding upon the other. If I were to ask you right now how your marriage is, you would probably answer me based on how it's working *for you*, how satisfied *your needs* are in your marriage, and how *you feel* about your husband. We gauge the health of our marriage by the degree our soul is satisfied, and we expect our spouse to be the one satisfying those needs.

Single ladies, widows, divorcees, pardon me, if you will. But I really need to have a word with our married sisters for a couple of days. I hate the idea of excluding you from even a day of Bible study, so I ask you to please study along with us. But there may be an occasional question that you have to leave blank due to the nature of the subject. Please don't be offended. If a better understanding of the marriage relationship weren't so crucial to this study, I would refrain from going there, but it is. And obviously many of you have either been married and/or one day will be, so please study right along with us married gals. These two lessons may certainly come in handy in your future or you may use this information to wisely counsel a married friend or family member one day.

Please read Genesis 2:18-25 in your Bible. If you will, underline every word or phrase in this section of scripture that describes the nature of the first man and woman's relationship. Summarize or list the words and phrases you underlined below the heading I've provided.

Man and Woman in Marriage (Genesis 2:18-25):

I have underlined "suitable helper", "bone of my bones", "flesh of my flesh", "one flesh", "leave", "cleave", and "naked and not ashamed" in my New American Standard Bible. From these phrases I gather that in the marriage relationship: the man and woman are suitable for one another, the woman was created so they could live in relationship and not alone, they are cut from the same cloth, they leave their parents and cleave to each other (they have an exclusive relationship), and they are able to be completely transparent with one another without shame. These phrases describe marriage as it was intended to be. Of course after sin enters the world through the actions of this man and woman a few things change.

Please read Genesis 3:8-24 in your Bible. Record the consequences of Adam and Eve's disobedience in the proper columns below.

The consequences of Adam and Eve's Sin:

The serpent:	The woman:	The ground:	The man:

Now that you've done the ground work on this important passage, I'd like to provide you with a few important statements that will help unlock a crucial concept for our marriages in regard to the subject matter of this Bible study.

- Only the serpent and the ground are *cursed*. God does not curse those He created in His image, the man and woman. He spells out consequences, but doesn't curse.

- God speaks to the woman in regards to her roles as a wife and a mother. These are the two roles, according to biblical thought, in which a woman experiences her highest fulfillment. Now there will be pain and frustration in these two areas.

- One commentator suggests that these verses (16-19) should not be read as prescriptions, but as descriptions of what life is like when separated from God, and their sin has, of course, now separated them from God.[4]

---

4   Walter A. Elwell, editor, *Evangelical Commentary on the Bible* (Grand Rapids, Michigan: 1989), p. 14.

- Notice that in Genesis 1:27-28 God had created the man and woman to co-rule over the created world, but now in chapter 3 the man rules over the woman. While it may have been God's intended order for the man to lead and for the woman to help, now that sin had entered the world the relationship would not operate so smoothly. Before, man would have ruled with wisdom and love and woman would have submitted with humility and meekness. Now their relationship would include selfishness, enmity, frustration and distrust.

- Most commentators believe the word "desire," used in Genesis 3:16 to describe the woman's feelings toward the man, infers that she would have an inordinate desire to rule over him, to master him. This desire would naturally frustrate the woman (and you and me) because the man would in fact rule the woman. Thus, when a woman tries to rule over her husband, the man's God-given need to rule is challenged and the man responds with frustration of some sort.

- Other commentators interpret the word "desire" in Genesis 3:16 to indicate that the woman (and her daughters) would long for a level of intimacy from her husband that he would not be able to give her because of his role as "ruler." She would be searching for something from her husband that the close, intimate relationship with her God had once provided.

- Yet another commentator has this to say about the woman's dilemma after her sin. "What is this desire the woman shall have to the husband? Simply, it is to replace that which she lost in the eating of the forbidden fruit. Her husband does not manifest the same love and adoration as before. The longing of her heart is to be the source of his happiness. Her focus is on the relationship the two of them have. She will be forever in need of assurances of his love, that she has regained the favour in his eyes in which she had taken such delight."[5]

- One commentator suggests these divine mandates are not God's way of "getting even" or "teaching a lesson," but are in fact gifts of love from God. He suggests these painful circumstances and the frustrations in the relationship are meant to *draw* men and women back to the God with whom they once enjoyed perfect fellowship.[6]

Now I'm going to ask you to do something a little unusual.

1. Please stop to pray, asking God to give you insight into your own marriage from the scriptures we have read today. Ask the Holy Spirit to open your mind to the deeper truths we might glean from this passage.
2. Read Genesis 2:18-25 and Genesis 3:8-24 again, carefully keeping in mind the commentary statements I gave you.
3. Answer the questions below.

---

5   James Dixon, Genesis: Expository Thoughts (Webster, New York: Evangelical Press, 2005), p. 98.
6   Elwell, p. 14.

1. If you are married, do you find yourself seeking a level of intimacy from your husband that he has a difficult time giving? Explain your answer.

2. Do you ever feel the need to win your husband's approval all over again? Do you fear losing his love and affection? Do you catch yourself trying to diagnose how he feels about you? Explain.

3. After today's study do you believe your husband is capable of meeting *all* your needs? Why or why not? To what extent do you believe, scripturally, you should hold him *responsible* for meeting *any* of your needs? In other words, should you be angry when he does not meet your legitimate needs for affection or companionship?

From our study in the book of beginnings, I believe we find that God did indeed create the first man and woman in such a way that they could have lived in perfect harmony with one another. He put them in a lush garden, gave them manageable responsibilities, supplied them with all they needed, and, most importantly, walked in sweet fellowship with them. He had taken care of every need, including physical, emotional and spiritual. He was the supplier of all of their needs.

But when sin entered the picture, that perfect set-up was destroyed. More importantly, their sin separated them from their God, the One who had met all of their needs. They had lost their intimate fellowship with God and they had also lost the atmosphere of complete satisfaction that He provided. Now they would live in frustration with each other, expecting each other to somehow do for them what their God had done and what only He *could* do.

Marriage is a spiritual union, one that was instituted by God for the purpose of relationship. When a man and a woman have been reunited with their God through the blood of Jesus Christ (the seed promised first in Genesis 3:15), they have the opportunity to create a fulfilling marriage that reflects closely on God's original plan for husband and wife. Why? Because the One who originally satisfied every need of Adam and Eve is now the one meeting every need for that redeemed couple. He is in the center of their union where He belongs and He is satisfying their souls, both individually and as a couple. Life is not perfect, as it was in the Garden of Eden, but intimacy with the Maker has been restored and now the husband and wife can love, support, respect, and help each other as they were meant to do.

But when one or both marriage partners either do not know God or refuse to look to Him to meet their needs, the frustration promised to Adam and Eve soon characterizes that marriage as well.

In what ways are you prone to look to your husband to meet your needs instead of seeking satisfaction completely and directly from God? What needs do you most often voice to him?

Instead of voicing those needs – for affection, conversation, help around the house, intimacy, whatever – to your husband, are you willing to try taking those needs directly and only to God for the next month? You could begin by pouring out your heart to God right here, right now.

Sweet sister, I am praying a blessing for your marriage today. But in that blessing I am asking that God help you to enjoy your husband as a source of blessing from Him rather than seeing him (your husband) as the one who is ultimately responsible for making you happy. No man can bear that burden. When we put our husbands under the weight of that unreasonable task, we simply set them up to fail. They struggle under the burden and eventually begin to resent the one who placed it on their shoulders. Believe me; I've been there – heaping the responsibility for my satisfaction on my husband. I'm married to a godly guy who would do anything within his power to please me, but he can't be my all in all. That responsibility and privilege is reserved for my God and He bears it well.

Day 3
But What about "His Needs Her Needs?"

When I first realized that biblically I was not supposed to be looking to my husband to meet my needs – to satisfy my soul – I had an immediate flashback to a book my husband and I had read just before we married. Willard F. Harley's book *His Needs Her Needs: Building an Affair-Proof Marriage* presents a list of ten emotional needs that the average person brings into a marriage. According to Mr. Harley if a couple does the necessary work to meet those needs for each other, then the marriage will be healthy and weather the storms ahead. But when those needs are unfulfilled, one or both partners will likely seek to have those needs met outside the marriage, resulting in an affair.

As I recalled, Mr. Harley advocated that there are five needs a woman has and five distinctly different needs ranked more highly by men. If I would meet my husband's needs for sexual fulfillment, recreational companionship, physical attractiveness, domestic support, and admiration, then he would be more likely to meet my needs for affection, conversation, honesty and openness, financial support, and family commitment. And if I didn't do my part to meet my husband's level of expectation, then I had no one to blame for my husband's potential infidelity but myself.

This made me angry.

I could have saved myself some frustration by rereading the book instead of assuming my memory served me well. Turns out, I wasn't recalling the book with a great degree of accuracy.

What Mr. Harley in fact says is that the *average* woman ranks her most pressing needs as 1) affection, 2) conversation, 3) honesty and openness, 4) financial support, and 5) family commitment. Likewise, he contends that years of working with couples heading toward divorce has shown him that the average man says he needs 1) sexual fulfillment, 2) recreational companionship, 3) physical attractiveness, 4) domestic support, and 5) admiration from his wife. The author, much to my surprise, acknowledges, however, that few folks are average so you have to assess your needs on a personal basis and make your spouse aware of them.

Mr. Harley also makes no guarantees that meeting your spouse's needs will result in him meeting yours. It is up to you to communicate your needs to your spouse in a loving way and to respond positively when he attempts to meet those needs. And of course Mr. Harley does not excuse infidelity even if a spouse's needs are not being met; he simply states that a spouse is more likely to go outside the marriage for satisfaction if he or she is not finding it within the relationship.

A simple perusal of the book cleared up those misconceptions, but one concern remained. I thought I had heard clearly from God and understood from scripture that He alone was responsible for meeting my needs, that I should not put that burden on my husband. And if I wasn't going to put that burden on him, then I didn't want him putting that responsibility on my shoulders either.

That's when I decided to do something we all should do when we encounter a teaching that, though it may sound wise and be substantiated with statistics and polls, does not quite ring true with Scripture. I decided to go back to the Bible and see what it has to say about me meeting my spouse's needs and him meeting mine.

Please read the following scriptures and list your findings in the appropriate columns.

Scripture Concerning Marriage:	How the Husband is to Satisfy His Wife or Meet Her Needs	How the Wife is to Satisfy Her Husband or Meet His Needs
1 Peter 3:1-2		
1 Peter 3:7		
Colossians 3:18-19		
Ephesians 5:22-33		

Scripture does indeed teach that a wife is to give her husband respect, which Mr. Harley, author of *His Needs Her Needs,* found to be one of the top five needs of most husbands. It also teaches that husbands are to give their wives love – love that is demonstrated by sacrifice and kind deeds as Christ demonstrates His love for us. Once again demonstrative love (affection) is listed in *His Needs Her Needs* as one of the average woman's top five needs. In fact, for many women this is *the* top need.

But what about the others needs Mr. Harley addresses in his book? Should a husband or wife expect their spouse to meet those needs? I believe part of the answer is found in the passage we looked at yesterday.

Read Genesis 2:24 below and underline the portions of the scripture that detail what a man and woman are to *do* when they enter into a marriage relationship.

For this cause a man shall leave his father and his mother, and shall cleave to his wife; and they shall become one flesh. (Genesis 2:24, NASB)

We all know what it means to leave, right? To leave means to walk away from, part from, exit from. But what does it mean to cleave? According to the *Vine's Complete Expository Dictionary of Old and New Testament Words*, "cleave" is translated from the Hebrew word *dabaq*, which means "to cling, cleave, keep close." It also means "to stick to, adhere to." Vine continues, "*dabaq* yields the noun form for 'glue' and also the more abstract ideas of 'loyalty, devotion.'" Obviously the implications of this word are simply fleshed out in the third instruction which is to "become one flesh." The husband and wife are supposed to forsake all other loyalties to the point that they are now able to operate as one, with no opposing loyalties or dependencies pulling them apart.

If a husband and wife leave their parents and cleave to one another, becoming one, what are the implications for their relationship?

The marriage relationship is supposed to be an exclusive union. Because of its exclusivity, there are certain needs that are best met through each other instead of those needs being met by any other source. One such need, of course, is the physical need for sex. No one, absolutely no one else is supposed to meet that need. Hebrews 13:4 teaches us that sex outside of the marriage relationship is sin and will be judged by God, but sex within the marriage partnership is perfectly honorable.

Please read 1 Corinthians 7:1-5 in your Bible. What does this passage teach about your responsibility to meet your spouse's sexual needs?

In practical terms, what are the possible implications of not meeting your spouse's physical need for sex? What might happen if that need goes unmet by the spouse?

Because the marriage relationship is supposed to be mutually exclusive, can you see where it would be best for certain other needs to be met *mostly* through the marriage partner instead of through other people? Why or why not?

If a woman's top five needs are generally for affection, conversation, honesty and openness, financial support, and family commitment, through what channel do you think she should look for these needs to be met *most* of the time?

Beside each need, name the one or more channels through which you currently get this need met. I've started the first one for you and you can add to it (or cross out what doesn't apply to you) and continue on with the others.

Affection –   *husband, children, pets...*

Conversation –

Honesty and Openness –

Financial Support –

Family Commitment –

Now return to the lists you made above and circle the one channel you listed beside each need through which you get that need met *most* of the time. Be honest.

You may have glossed over the last need, family commitment, and assumed, "who else could I have that need met by except my husband?" But, sweet sister, if you've failed to really leave your mother or father as Genesis 2:24 commanded, you still may be getting your need satisfied more by one or both of your parents than by your husband. Likewise, you may be looking more to another source or even your own devices to have the need for financial support met. These are simply things to think about and pray about. The Bible doesn't specifically say I should be getting these "top five needs" met by my husband, but if I'm going to have a "leave and cleave" type of marriage, I believe it is probably best to give my husband the opportunity to be the channel through which God meets these needs at least *most* of the time. And many of us are, quite frankly, guilty of not even giving our husbands a fighting chance to meet those needs, and then we complain and run to other sources.

And that brings us to the final point of today's lesson. I still contend that you and I will be healthier, happier, more contented wives if we continue to look completely to Jesus, the Bread of Life, to meet our every need rather than putting that burden on our husbands.

Please read Exodus 16:1-12 in your Bible and answer the following questions.

1. What were the people of Israel doing in verse 2? Be specific.

2. Using your biblical knowledge, did Moses and Aaron have some degree of responsibility for the people of Israel? Why do you answer as you do?

3. What did Moses and Aaron say would be the results of God's provision in verses 6 and 7?

4. What is Moses' and Aaron's question for the people in verse 7?

5. Who does Moses say the peoples' grumblings are really directed toward in verse 8?

6. What is God's response to the peoples' grumblings according to verse 12?

Sweet sister, if your husband is not meeting one of your "top five needs" or any other need that you think is legitimate but lacking, don't grumble against him the way the Israelites did toward Moses and Aaron. Yes, your husband is certainly in a position where he is responsible to meet some of your needs and he is the best person through whom God could choose to meet some of those needs. But ultimately God *is* and *wants to be* responsible for all of your needs. I believe God wanted the people to respect Moses and even look to him as the channel through which God would provide for them. But obviously God wanted His people to go to *Him* with their every need. Likewise, your God wants you to voice your needs to Him. Certainly you can calmly and respectfully let your husband know what you would like out of your marriage relationship and then you can, and should, ask him how you can better meet his needs. But many of us have gotten into the bad habit of blaming our husbands for our dissatisfaction, and grumbling just perpetuates bad feelings, resentments, and bitterness.

I have found that if I look to my husband as simply a *channel* or a *vessel* through which God blesses me and meets my needs I am much more prone to keep a soft heart toward his shortcomings than I would if I put the *burden* of meeting my needs on his shoulders. This attitude has been the key to making our relationship one in which grace abounds instead of one in which bitterness grows. I try to *allow* my husband to meet many of my emotional needs so I don't go looking for those needs to be met elsewhere, but I *expect* God to meet my needs.

How might it change your marriage if you put the responsibility for satisfying your needs on God and simply allowed Him to use your husband as a channel for those provisions instead of putting that expectation on your man?

I do have one final comment. The purpose of this lesson is not to "let you off the hook" when it comes to meeting your husband's needs. Instead you can now see yourself as a channel of God's blessings in his life as well. Hopefully with our focus off of how our husbands ought to be meeting our needs, we can now be more intentional about making ourselves available to God as vessels through which He can meet the needs of others, including and especially the needs of our husbands.

◢

Day 4
Filled Up to Pour Out

When I fill my washing machine with cold, soapy water it's so I can wash my family's clothes. If I fill a pitcher with fresh, pink lemonade it's so I can quench my guests' thirst with something sweet and refreshing. I only put fuel in my car so the car can take me where I need to go. And I if I load my refrigerator up with yogurt, fruit, veggies, and cold drinks, I hope my family will reach into my well-stocked fridge when they need a snack or a simple meal. Do you see where I'm going with this?

We fill things up in order to put them to use. While a young child may fill a bucket with blocks just for the fun of it, I can't think of a single thing that we "fill up" with something for no reason at all. Can you?

Complete the following sentences.

We fill a swimming pool with water in order to...

We fill our drawers with clothes so we can...

We fill an IPod with music so we can...

We fill a classroom with students in order to...

We fill a library with books so people can...

God fills a soul with His gracious, satisfying abundance so she can...

I'm curious to know how you completed that last sentence. That is the focus of today's lesson. Indeed, God fills us to satisfaction for a reason. I believe a clue is provided in John chapter 4 to help us begin to understand what the reason is.

We've studied this passage before, but let's start at the beginning to regain our frame of reference. Please read John 4:7-15 in your Bible. Then fill in the blanks for John 4:14b below.

"...but the water that I shall _____ him shall become in him a _____ of water _____ _____ to eternal life." (John 4:14b, NASB)

Jesus told the Samaritan woman He could provide water that would not only quench her thirst, but that would spring up like an abundant fountain within her.

Draw a picture illustrating how this abundant, living water would look in a person's life.

Jesus is telling this tired, searching woman that He can satisfy all of her needs with abundance and even supply enough for her to share with others. This living water will well up, spring forth and splash out! Imagine how delightful and refreshing that must have sounded to this weary woman who had been looking for satisfaction in all the wrong men, um, I mean wrong places. I wonder how good it sounds to you too.

If Jesus is willing to satisfy our thirsts with more than enough living water, then He obviously means for us to use it. Not only should that abundance allow us the joy of splashing around in the overflow a little (and I'm all for that!), but we should be willing to pour out of our abundance into the lives of others. In fact, later in this same passage we see that in the pouring out to others, we are indeed satisfied all the more.

Please back up and read John 4:3-8 in your Bible. Answer the following questions.

1. What is Jesus' physical condition as described in verse 6?

2. Approximately what time is it?

3. Where have the disciples gone and for what purpose?

Please read John 4:16-42 in your Bible. Answer the following questions.

1. Why did the woman leave her waterpot and run back to her city?

2. What have the disciples obviously brought to Jesus at this point? What do they want him to do? (vs. 31)

3. Why is Jesus no longer all that interested in the food? What had satisfied His hunger?

Obviously, Jesus is not advocating that we minister with no regard for our physical needs, but His comment to the disciples must not be wasted on us either. He is turning down the food for which He was surely hungry because He is so full of something much better. He is literally feasting on the fruits of His labor. Even though He was already spent to the point of weariness, Jesus ministered truth and compassion to the Samaritan woman. He did the work the Father had appointed Him to do and the result was such soul satisfaction that even His stomach stopped growling. Do you almost hear the lift in Jesus' voice as you read through John chapter 4? Do you hear the weariness in His voice as He sits at the well and says to the woman, "Give me a drink" in verse 7? Do you hear the excitement grow and the passion being restored as He tells her about the living water He offers? Do you sense that Jesus is no longer sitting down, but standing up, fully refreshed and ready to get back to work in verses 35-37?

I don't know if Jesus ever received water from the Samaritan woman. And I'm not sure he ever ate the food the disciples brought Him from town. But He got His fill of soul satisfying heavenly manna when He did the work the Father had sent Him to do.

According to John 4:41-42, what was the result of Jesus willingly pouring out?

The ultimate purpose for which God satisfies our hungry souls is for us to share the gospel with those around us. When we can give testimony to the fullness He supplies us, we indeed have good news to share with a hurting world. And it is often with remembrance of our point of deepest need that we can best relate to the people around us.

Recently I have heard two wonderful testimonies presented in the worship services at my church. Both testimonies were given by women who came to know Jesus out of desperate need. Both Mary and Quinn told stories of how they had hit rock bottom through their own sinful lifestyles. By their own accounts, they were searching for something to satisfy their souls in all the wrong places – alcohol, drugs, illicit relationships, money, possessions. By the time either of these women came to Jesus they were cloaked in shame and regret. But when Jesus came into their lives and filled their souls as only He could, they were changed forever. And neither Mary nor Quinn has been quiet about their changed lives since the day they each met the Lover of their souls. God didn't just change them for their own benefit; He did a mighty work in their lives so they would bring Him glory and honor. And He didn't just fill their hungry souls so they could lick their lips with satisfaction; He filled them so they could pour out that overflowing well of eternal life to others. And that's exactly what they're doing.

I was so blessed by Mary's and Quinn's testimonies. They both gave concise and relatable stories of what their lives were like before they met Jesus, how they encountered Jesus and He satisfied their souls, and how their lives have been different ever since. They related to those who were still without Jesus, gave crystal clear explanations of how they met Him, and gave hope-filled testimonies of how full their lives have been because of Jesus. Mary and Quinn were simply and beautifully pouring out what God had poured in, and as a result everyone who heard their stories was able to drink in that cool, sweet refreshment and praise the Lord along with them.

1. Name a time in your life when you found yourself at a point of great need. What soul hunger caused you to either find Jesus for the very first time or drove you to search for Him like never before?

2. How did Jesus satisfy that particular hunger? Describe as fully as you can how Jesus answered you and met that need.

3. How has life been different since Jesus satisfied your soul? What difference did the Bread of Life make in your life?

Dear friend, you have just written out your personal testimony of how Jesus has satisfied your soul. I guarantee you someone in your sphere of influence needs to hear your story. Your place of hunger (question #1) is what makes your story relatable. Your answer to question #2 is what tells people how they, too, can have their souls satisfied by Jesus Christ. And your answer to #3 is what whets their appetite for a soul-quenching taste of that living water. Please don't miss the opportunities He gives you for sharing your own personal message of hunger turned to satisfaction. You were filled for a purpose. And when you fulfill that purpose you'll find that even the fruit of your labor satisfies you more than food or water.

⌒M⌒

Day 5
The Miraculous Effects of Pouring Out

Yesterday we concluded that Jesus fills us up for the purpose of using us to glorify God, edify the saints, and save the lost. We are also filled up for the simple purpose of ministry. Of course ministry or service can take all sorts of forms.

Give yourself 60 seconds to name as many avenues of ministry as you can. Simply jot down every type of service you can think of in one minute. The sky's the limit!

Now, if that little exercise didn't exhaust you, actually doing any of those ministries you listed certainly can. Ministry is hard work. Service is all about putting yourself aside at least momentarily and doing whatever it takes to meet someone else's need. And in my experience, most people don't need simple things. Meeting their needs often requires that I get my hands dirty, sometimes means going the distance, frequently means doling out the big bucks, and usually includes no small forfeiture of my time. Ministry is costly...and draining.

Ministry isn't just the stuff you do at the church either. You minister to your family when you take care of them and meet their daily needs. You minister to your husband when you listen to him, watch a football game with him, or take him a glass of lemonade as he paints the back deck. You minister to your parents when you send them pictures of the grandkids, invite them to visit, or call long-distance for a chat. And you minister to your neighbor when you invite them to a cookout, gather their mail while they're out of town, or mow their grass just because. For many of us, if God has filled us to the point of soul-satisfying saturation, ministry is a welcomed way of life.

But it's also a responsibility. Funny thing, but I've noticed that as long as ministry is just an afterthought or voluntary gift, it actually refreshes us to serve. We walk back from our neighbor's house with a bounce in our step or we serve our husband with a smile. But when ministry becomes a responsibility, it often takes on a different feel. That's when it becomes weighty, draining, and tiring.

In the chart below list two or three of your biggest *responsibilities* in the left hand column. I've provided one of my own as an example.

Responsibility:	What tires or drains you about this responsibility:	What living water would look like:
Taking care of my home	*The repetition of laundry, dishes, feeding dogs. Doing most of it by myself while working too. Feeling like I never get it all done.*	*Energy to finish the job, motivation to do it well, joy in doing yet another load of laundry, focus on the people I'm doing it for, perspective.*

In the center column describe what about each responsibility tires or drains you.

In the final column, describe what living water would look like as it applies to that responsibility. If Jesus were to give you water resembling "a well of water springing up to eternal life" so that you could splash in its abundance rather than feeling drained, what would that water "taste" or "feel" like for you in regard to that responsibility?

Has serving your family ever left you feeling depleted and needy at the end of the day? Has the ministry you signed up for at church and really love doing ever left you feeling weary with the weight of responsibility? Do you feel passionate about helping out at your child's school, but occasionally dread putting in the time? Or maybe you have the extra responsibility of a sick parent, a wounded child returned to the nest, a struggling sibling, or a grieving best friend. Maybe, like many of the women I minister to each week, you're keeping the home fires burning as brightly as you can while your spouse is deployed and the "single parent" load is about to take you under.

When you are *required* to pour out day after day after long day because that is your current responsibility, it is easy to begin to feel like you are operating on empty. And you may have done everything I've suggested up to this point in the Bible study, and yet still fear that if things don't let up, even a daily diet of the Bread of Life will not have any sticking power.

Don't give up hope sweet young mama, dutiful daughter, loving spouse, generous friend, single parent, mother of a child with special needs, parent of a wayward teen, military wife. There is hope for those who are required to pour out even more than their fair share.

Please read 1 Chronicles 29:1-18 in your Bible. Mark the following words with your colored pencils or using distinguishing symbols:
- God, Lord, applicable pronouns
- work, task
- my ability, my resources
- provided
- the house of my God, the temple of my God
- offered, offering, gave, given (depending on your translation)
- willingly
- Thy (Your) hand
- heart

This passage provides us a glimpse into David's heart as he both contemplates the enormity of the task of building a temple for God and rejoices in the willing generosity of his people. You'll remember that David wanted desperately to build a permanent dwelling place for the Spirit of God, but God gave the privilege and responsibility to his son Solomon. Still David has been able to draw up the plans for the temple, gather the materials needed, and line up the overseers for the intricate work that must be done. In this passage you undoubtedly noticed that David is both overwhelmed by the responsibility and cost of the task and amazed that the people have been able to accomplish as much as they have. More work lies ahead and Solomon is young. Will he be able to handle the responsibility God has given him? According to David's summation, yes, if and only if he acknowledges that all the resources begin and end with God.

1. According to what you read, how would you describe the impending work that needed to be done?

2. To what degree has David given towards the massive project?

3. When David extended an invitation to the rest of Israel to participate in the building of the temple through "consecrating themselves" or giving of themselves to the task (vs. 5), what was their response?

4. As they gave of their resources, *how* did they give?

5. Look over David's words of praise and acknowledgment in verses 10-15 once again. According to David, how were the people able to give so sacrificially and yet so willingly?

6. Lest you think that God simply supplies financial and tangible resources like gold and silver, what kind of resources does 1 Chronicles 29:11-12 say God is the supplier of? List each one you find.

7. Finally, according to David's insight (from a man who has a heart after God's own heart), what is the key to the people's service in God's eyes? (see verses 17-18)

God supplies all we need so we can do the work He's called us to do. He will never call you to do something or give you a responsibility for which He also does not equip you. And He doesn't just equip you with the skills, the finances, and the know-how. Not only does He supply the strength, the power, the victory, or whatever fiber of fortitude you may require to do the job and do it with a song in your heart, He also holds the strength you need to carry on and the power you need to finish the job well. Ask Him for it, dear sister. He gives generously to those who are willing to turn around and pour out generously to others.

Not convinced? I have one last gem of a scripture that will knock the socks right off your exhausted feet! Get your 4x6 index cards out because you'll want to add this one to your memory book. It's a winner, especially if you're in one of those very demanding, very draining places of service right now. In fact, before we go to this scripture, let's voice our need honestly before God so this word of truth can wash over us like a healing balm applied to an open wound.

Please voice to God your greatest frustrations about the heaviest responsibility you are carrying right now. Honestly tell Him what is wearing you out and what is depleting you.

Now, read Isaiah 58:10 -11 below.
- **Underline the words that detail your responsibility.**
- **Circle the supernatural side effects of drinking from the living water and eating the Bread of Life as you give to others.**
- **Put boxes around the words that detail what God will do for you if you obediently, generously, and willingly pour out what He pours in.**

> And if you give yourself to the hungry,
> And satisfy the desire (soul) of the afflicted,
> Then your light will rise in the darkness,
> And your gloom will become like midday.
> And the Lord will continually guide you,
> And satisfy your desire (soul) in scorched places,
> And give strength to your bones;
> And you will be like a watered garden,
> And like a spring of water whose waters do not fail.
> Isaiah 58:10-11 (NASB)

Write these verses on an index card and add it to your scripture album. If you are in an extreme service intensive time in your life, I suggest you meditate on this scripture daily.

Father,

Thank you for giving me opportunities to pour out Your love to those around me. But to be honest, sometimes all the pouring leaves me exhausted and drained. I don't want my praises to turn into bitter complaints, and I don't want to run so dry that I go running back to those dry cisterns that I frequented before. So I lift up my water jar to You alone and I ask You, in this season of extreme demand, to supply all that I need, not only to keep me full, but to keep me overflowing. I want my life to be characterized as a "watered garden." I want others to see that the spring of living water that fuels my life indeed does not fail. Make my life a testimony of your generous provision and I will give you all the praise and all the glory. Amen.

Week 5

Discussion Questions

1. Kay said the ultimate goal of having our souls satisfied through Jesus is to then turn our attention outward so we can share the love of God with others. She contends that contentment should lead to less self-absorption and more compassion and concern for others. Do you agree? Why or why not?

2. If a friend asked you how they could "learn" to be content, how would you answer them? What do you think is involved in learning to be content?

3. Share what you have determined to be hot buttons of discontentment for you (Day 1) and how you plan to steer clear of those things in order to practice contentment.

4. Have you ever been frustrated with your husband because your needs were not being met? How did your directing your frustration towards him affect your marriage relationship?

5. How does it change your marriage if you view your spouse as a channel through which God can meet your needs rather than seeing your spouse as the one who is *responsible* for those needs?

6. Jesus said His food was accomplishing the work the Father had sent Him to do. Doing that work satisfied Him more than the food the disciples brought to him. Tell about a time when doing God's work satisfied you.

7. For what purpose have you been filled up and satisfied? What huge hunger or scorching thirst has God satisfied in you that you could tell others about?

8. How do the promises of Isaiah 58:10-11 affect you? To what weighty responsibility have you applied these scriptures?

Week 6 – The Land of Milk & Honey

This week our lessons will continue to focus on learning to be content. I hope you understand that we don't have to *learn* contentment because that which God provides is less than abundant. Far from it. We have to learn to be content because our eyes continue to stray to that which is pleasing to the eye, our ears continue to entertain the subtle but deceptive voice of the evil one, our noses continue to sniff out the familiar odors of our former diet, and our mouths continue to salivate for that which may have tasted good but later proved to be dangerously poisonous.

Join me this final week of study on a journey to the wilderness area between Egypt and Canaan. We'll walk alongside the nation of Israel, God's chosen people, as they leave a land where they had indeed been fed, but at great cost. They had paid a pricey toll for food that was rationed out by a cruel slave master instead of provided freely by a loving God. We'll learn the lessons of finding contentment and satisfaction with the manna from heaven while journeying toward the land of milk and honey. And we'll consider one final penetrating question: What if I'm still hungry?

Throughout the story of the Israelites' pilgrimage, God uses the imagery of food and water to explain His willingness to satisfy His people's every need. Most every time He promises to satisfy their hunger or thirst, He is also promising to satisfy their souls. Unfortunately the people of Israel had a difficult time grasping that concept and they continued again and again to doubt His ability to provide—for their stomachs, much less for their souls. May the final leg of our journey together result in a better learning curve!

Day 1
Is Your Mouth Still Watering?

When Jacob, or Israel as God renamed him, and his family first went to Egypt during a time of famine, they were welcomed and esteemed because of their relationship to Joseph. But 430 years later when the people of Israel had become more of a nation than a family (as God had promised Abraham), Pharaoh began to fear them and subjected them to hard labor, the cruel annihilation of their baby boys, and harsh treatment from their taskmasters.

How did the Israelites' predicament in Egypt parallel our situations when we have developed co-dependencies, addictions or coping mechanisms for getting our fill? Name at least two similarities if you can. You might read Exodus 1:1-14 for insight.

1.

2.

3.

The family of Israel had moved to Egypt during a time of famine in order to have food to eat. The king of Egypt took them in willingly and provided bounty for them. But as time passed, their place of refuge turned into a place of captivity. While the family of Israel had moved to Egypt in order to satisfy their stomachs during a time of famine, they now found themselves in bondage to the very hand that had fed them. Sound familiar?

When Israel finally directed their cries of desperation to the God of their fathers, He heard them and sent a deliverer to bring them out of their slavery. He selected Moses, both an Israelite haunted by the oppression of his people and an Egyptian prince living on the backside of nowhere, to set His people free. Moses argued with God at first, but finally agreed to approach Pharaoh about the release of Israel.

Read Exodus 3:16-17 below and circle the portion of the scripture that details that from which God desired to deliver the Israelites.

"Go and gather the elders of Israel together, and say to them, 'The Lord, the God of your fathers, the God of Abraham, Isaac and Jacob, has appeared to me, saying, "I am indeed concerned about you and what has been done to you in Egypt. So I said, I will bring you up out of the affliction of Egypt to the land of the Canaanite and the Hittite and the Amorite and the Perizzite and the Hivite and the Jebusite, to a land flowing with milk and honey."'" (Exodus 3:16-17, NASB)

Please read Exodus 1:8-14 in your Bible. Record every phrase or word that indicates how tough the Egyptians were on the Israelites, and cite the appropriate scripture references. I'll start.

taskmasters (vs. 11)
afflict them with hard labor (vs. 11)

Many of you who have accompanied me on this Bible study journey have also identified places of oppression and bondage in your life. You, like me, have realized that some of the places you went to for soul satisfaction have turned against you. While they may have satisfied you for a while, they later became taskmasters of affliction. While you were dependent on the "food" they could provide, they required more and more of you in order to provide even a semblance of satisfaction.

Whether you identified such a situation of bondage in your own life or not, can you name three types of relationships, substances or experiences that often initially satisfy and then potentially turn into nasty taskmasters?

1.

2.

3.

You may have named a few of the "biggies" like drinking alcohol, smoking, viewing pornography, or doing drugs, but let's remember that the sky is the limit when it comes to possible taskmasters. Without proper boundaries, relationships can become sticky and manipulative. Substances of all sorts – drugs, alcohol, cigarettes, food, caffeine, sugar, etc. – can demand more and more allegiance from you. And even experiences such as shopping, exercising, taking risks, winning competitions, surfing the Internet, or gambling can turn from innocent pastimes into compulsive behaviors that won't let you go when you're ready to move on. And, as a final and humiliating blow, any of these things can claim you as their captor and convince you there is no hope. In the same way, Egypt had hundreds of thousands of Israelites persuaded that they were helpless slaves, your co-dependencies can strip you of your self-esteem and make you think you have no choice but to keep tirelessly working to earn your soul's pitiful daily dose of satisfaction.

Hopefully, at this point in our study, you have begun the hard work of breaking free from those things, people or experiences that may have kept you captive while you tried to suck one more drop of satisfaction from their wells. Hopefully you have seen them for the broken cisterns they are, picked up your water jar, and walked away. If not, I encourage you to walk away today with the Israelites as they leave Egypt in their dust.

The Israelites did follow Moses out of their land of captivity, their place of oppression. But when they left Egypt they suddenly realized they had quite a journey before them and the route God was taking them didn't lead immediately to the Promised Land. Complete and total satisfaction was not just around the block and to the left. They would have to walk many miles to the land of milk and honey, and as they travelled they would need to learn to depend on and go to a new provider, Jehovah-Jireh, the God Who Provides.

In the wilderness that stretched between Egypt and Canaan there was no milk or honey. In fact, a few times the Israelites were led by God to pitch their tents in places that even lacked water or adequate sources of food. We know from previous lessons that they expressed their displeasure over their lack of resources by murmuring and grumbling against Moses and Aaron. While this round-about communication did not please God, He did provide for their needs by causing water to flow from a rock, sweetening the water that at first tasted bitter, sending quail and providing manna from heaven. Not a very elaborate diet, but definitely sufficient.

Still, as the people adjusted to their new life of freedom, they tended to look over their shoulders at what they'd left behind, especially when the going got tough.

As you've learned to go to Jesus to have all of your soul needs met instead of looking to other sources for that satisfaction, what sometimes prompts you to look back?

Read Numbers 11:4-6 below. Circle the foods the Israelites had left behind.

"The rabble who were among them had greedy desires; and also the sons of Israel wept again and said, 'Who will give us meat to eat? We remember the fish which we used to eat free in Egypt, the cucumbers and the melons and the leeks and the onions and the garlic, but now our appetite is gone.'" (Numbers 11:4-6, NASB)

Funny how the Israelites did not remember everything quite as it actually was. They had not, in fact, eaten freely. They had instead been forced to work harder and harder for that which met their needs. They may have been exposed to a variety of foods, but at what cost? And they probably did know each day that they would indeed have food to eat. But don't you suppose the Egyptian taskmasters wanted the Israelites well-fed not so they would be happy and content, but so they would be fortified for the work to which they were enslaved? They were remembering the perks of their bondage without recalling the price they paid for those benefits.

As we break free from the codependent relationships, the addictions, the bad habits, and the coping mechanisms that once fed our souls, we will undoubtedly begin to miss the perks of our own Egypts too. We'll get a whiff of those things that tasted good at the time even if they soured in our stomachs later. We'll remember the taste of those things that tantalized our palate, but left us hungry, unsatisfied, and even sick with disgust. If we're not well aware of our tendency to glamorize our former captivity, just as the Israelites did, we'll go running right back to those strong flavors and odors only to find them just as deceptive as before. And the price for those familiar foods may be even higher the second time around.

Describe how the strong flavors and odors of the food they ate in Egypt might have made it even harder for them to put their place of bondage behind them. How might this tendency apply to you?

What substances, types of relationships, or experiences would you assume would be most indelibly etched into the senses so a person would remember them with fondness the way the Israelites longed for the strong and vibrant flavors of their Egyptian foods?

Consider some of the foods you've removed from your Soul Food pantry or relabeled for appropriate use.

- In the left hand column name the "food."
- In the center column describe the price you paid to satisfy your soul with that food.
- In the right hand column describe the "perk" of consuming that food. What tasted or smelled good about it, even if only temporarily?
- I'll get you started with an example.

Forsaken "Food":	Price paid:	How it tasted or smelled good:
Alcohol	*Couldn't stop; lost integrity; affected my behavior poorly; it consumed me, caused me to make unwise decisions.*	*Relaxed me; social thing to do; made me feel adult and sophisticated; tasted good*

More than likely each of the "perks" you listed in the right hand column – the sweet tastes or the savory smells – were things that fed the flesh, not the soul. The enemy seeks to feed the flesh because our flesh is what serves him well.

Read Galatians 5:16-25 in your Bible. If you feed the flesh, what happens? What fruit is produced by well-fed flesh?

The Bread of Life, on the other hand, satisfies the soul and feeds the Spirit. When you feast on the healthy Bread of Life it's like eating high fiber bread. It's filling and it allows the Spirit (the living water) to flow freely through you, producing the fruit of the Spirit.

According to Galatians 5:22-23, what is the healthy fruit of the Spirit produced by a well-fed soul?

Please read 1 Peter 2:11 below and underline the phrase that indicates the dilemma between the flesh and the soul.

"Beloved, I urge you as aliens and strangers to abstain from fleshly lusts, which wage war against the soul."

Dear sister, it will not be easy to deny the hungers of the flesh as we continue our journey toward Promised Land living. Your flesh will continue to cry out for that which you have walked away from, reminding you of the savory delights and the aromatic morsels you have determined to be unworthy of the price. Engage in the battle, determine to stand firm, and follow the advice of 1 Peter 2:16: Act as free men!

Write 1 Peter 2:11 on a 4x6 index card and add it to your scripture memory album.

One last question about Numbers 11:4-6: Who does it appear led the chorus of complaint? Who got the Israelites to thinking about the foods they'd left behind?

The "rabble who were among them" in Numbers 11:4 refers to any Egyptians or foreigners who had left Egypt with the Israelites – possibly slaves from other countries or Egyptian prisoners who were forced into slavery. These were not people who worshiped the true God, but simply those who were tagging along for the ride. But their memories of what they'd left behind, their greedy desires and their complaints stirred up the discontent of the Israelites.

Who would the "rabble" be in our lives as we leave behind that which did not satisfy in order to follow Jesus to our land of milk and honey? What could their affect be on us?

Sweet sister, we've begun the hard work of forsaking those things which do not really satisfy the soul. But more hard work remains. As we journey toward the abundant, soul-satisfying land of promise, we will be tempted to return to that from which we've broken free. In difficult times specifically, when the land seems especially parched and our daily bread is literally only being supplied one day at a time, we may recall the strong aromas or the tantalizing tastes of those pricey sources of satisfaction with a less-than-accurate memory. During such times we must choose to remember correctly, speak truth to our souls (from our Scripture memory books), and pray for the courage and strength to keep walking toward our Promised Land. We must commit to eating only from Jesus' soul food menu and resist the temptation to even salivate over the memories of things forsaken.

Day 2
Satisfaction & Abundance

When I first began to go to Jesus exclusively to have my soul needs satisfied I was skeptical that a God I couldn't see or touch or hear could actually bring me the kind of joy and fulfillment I was looking for. I understood how He could initiate it, how He could coordinate it, or how He could meet some needs, the really spiritual ones. But I didn't see how He alone could really fill me up to the point of overflowing abundance. I not only wanted to be ok, adequately provided for, or properly nourished, I wanted to be giddy with life. I wanted the thrill of it all. Could He possibly give me all of that... all by Himself?

I might have thrown in the towel on the whole experiment except for the fact that God seemed to anticipate my doubts and He went to great lengths to limit my options; thus, I had nothing to "eat" *except* the Bread of Life. Friendships were minimized as I moved 900 miles away from close friends and I struggled to make new ones. My parents were even further away, my husband became busy with a new pastorate, and my children couldn't feed me because of their own neediness. In addition, the ministry and work in which I thrived was put on the back burner. God seemed to be stripping me of all sources of "food." Even the things that were healthy and wholesome were seemingly taken from me. Instead of feasting at a table, any table, it felt more like I was hooked up to an I.V. dispenser with the slow steady drip of just enough sustenance to survive.

And at first I did *just* survive. Many days I wondered how I was going to keep my head up, how I was going to get out of bed and do the things I needed to do. It was definitely a wilderness season for me, something akin to the journey the Israelites made from Egypt to Canaan. But just as God had a purpose in trimming the Israelites' menu as they traveled to their Promised Land, He also had a few things He was trying to teach me as I journeyed to a place of abundant life.

Please read Deuteronomy 8:3, 7-18 in your Bible. List every lesson God hoped the Israelites would learn from their experience in the wilderness and from the basic food He provided.

Considering the lessons God stated He wanted to teach Israel through their wilderness journey, what lessons might He have in store for us as we first learn to trust Him exclusively to fulfill our soul's desires?

When we first forsake our places of bondage and seek to have our hunger and thirst met by Jesus instead, we may find ourselves confined to what seems to be a rather limited menu. The enemy may have been providing you with a tantalizing variety, a wicked buffet of tasty morsels. But God wants us to learn to eat from one source for our satisfaction. He wants us to understand that we don't have to go from one person to another, one experience to another or one substance to another with our empty cups held out for a taste of this and a bite of that. Jesus alone can satisfy our souls, just like manna alone would satisfy the Israelites. God does not limit our soul diets to be mean and restrictive. He has a purpose and a plan that is loving and ultimately results in freedom.

Reread Deuteronomy 8:10-14. What potential problem is God concerned about as the Israelites begin to enjoy the abundance He provides?

God wants us to enjoy Him and our relationship with Him more than we enjoy the blessings He provides. But we are so apt to fall in love with the good stuff of life rather than the good God who provides it. Thus, God limited the Israelites' intake of good stuff for a while. He did the same for me.

Please read John 6:30-35, 47-51. What does Jesus liken Himself to in these verses?

In these scriptures Jesus infers that "eating Him," the Bread of Life, is the one way to live and never die. How does that truth relate to the fact that the Israelites had nothing to eat but manna for much of their journey to Canaan? Conversely, what does the Israelites' daily diet of manna teach us about how we get to our Promised Land?

If Jesus, the Bread of Life, compares Himself to the manna God sent from heaven, maybe we should understand a little more about that manna. I always assumed that since the Israelites complained about it so much, it must have been terrible. But I'm not so sure now.

Check out the scripture below and underline what you learn about the manna.

> Now the manna was like coriander seed, and its appearance like that of bdellium. The people would go about and gather it and grind it between two millstones or beat it in the mortar, and boil it in the pot and make cakes with it; and its taste was as the taste of cakes baked with oil. (Numbers 11:7-8)

After reading Numbers 11:7-8, manna sounds like the answer to my daily dilemma of what to cook for dinner! It was actually pleasing to the eye. It looked like bdellium, a treasured item that was originally found surrounding the Garden of Eden (Genesis 2:12).

Vine's Expository Dictionary of Old and New Testament Words says the word manna can be translated "what is it?" Fitting enough. Neither the Israelites nor their ancestors had ever seen or eaten such a food. It was indeed brand new and unique.

Draw lines connecting the scriptures with the corresponding truths we learn about manna.

Exodus 16:31   called bread of angels, served in abundance

Psalm 78:24   called spiritual food or spiritual meat

Psalm 78:25   called the bread of heaven

Psalm 105:40   it tasted like wafers with honey

1 Corinthians 10:3   called food or grain from heaven

Other translations interpret the words of Numbers 11 to say that it "tasted like a fine pastry cooked with the finest oil." Imagine your favorite treat at Starbuck's and you will have a pretty good idea of the taste of manna. The Israelites may have had to endure a daily diet of manna, but they couldn't claim to be eating second-class fixings. Today there are people who would give anything for a bowl of unflavored rice; and yet the people of God complained about eating fine pastries.

You and I have no reason to complain about eating heavenly bread each day either. We just need to learn to appreciate it for what it is – soul satisfying goodness sent straight from heaven and without the harmful side effects of other foods.

If Jesus is the bread of life that the Father has sent from heaven, we must believe that He can completely satisfy our every need and go to Him to have those needs met. We must believe Him when He says, "He who comes to Me shall not hunger, and he who believes in Me shall never thirst." (John 6:35)

Name some foods you sometimes eat when you're hungry but they don't really satisfy. Why do they not completely satisfy you?

That's not Jesus! You feast on Him and you get that wonderful "ahhh" feeling. You experience fullness! You are satisfied because the soul food you ate tasted good, smelled delicious, settled nicely in your soul, and is good for you. He is indeed adequate to satisfy us completely. And we do not have to look for supplemental food from any other source.

Read Exodus 3:16-17 and underline the portion of the scripture that details the kind of land God promised Israel if they would leave Egypt and follow Him.

"Go and gather the elders of Israel together, and say to them, 'The Lord, the God of your fathers, the God of Abraham, Isaac and Jacob, has appeared to me, saying, "I am indeed concerned about you and what has been done to you in Egypt. So I said, I will bring you up out of the affliction of Egypt to the land of the Canaanite and the Hittite and the Amorite and the Perizzite and the Hivite and the Jebusite, to a land flowing with milk and honey."'" (Exodus 3:16-17, NASB)

You're probably familiar with the phrase, "a land flowing with milk and honey." But have you ever really stopped to think about what that means?

How would you describe milk? What type of nourishment does it supply?

How would you describe honey?

Milk is a byproduct of animal husbandry. Milk would only be available in Canaan if animals were able to thrive there. Honey, though produced by bees, is actually a byproduct of prolific horticulture. Thus, fruit producing trees and vineyards would also flourish in Canaan. The "land flowing with milk and honey" would be a place of prosperity, abundance, and healthy life.

Also, milk is a staple, is it not? Ask the mother of any newborn baby and she will tell you that her baby *must* have milk to grow and the child craves it desperately. Milk is a required minimum for survival. Honey, on the other hand, is what makes life sweet. It is a luxury.

Could it be that God was promising the people a life of abundance? A life where all of their needs – both the most basic and the most extravagant – would be met? Could He have been promising them He would not only satisfy their basic needs, but would in fact make life extravagantly sweet? Let's check a New Testament promise that parallels God's offer to the Israelites for clarification.

"The thief comes only to steal, and kill, and destroy; I (Jesus) came that they might have life, and might have it abundantly." (John 10:10, NASB)

What two things does Jesus want to provide?

Do you see a correlation between what Jesus came to provide for you and me and the land flowing with milk and honey? Explain.

I believe Christ followers have the opportunity to live "milk and honey" lives every day. Because we are no longer waiting for the Messiah to come, but are celebrating His life, death, resurrection, and promised return, we can live in the Promised Land of abundance today. The abundant life Jesus promised doesn't begin one day; it is made available now.

Name some specific ways that life in Christ is similar to the life Israel was promised in Canaan. I'll get you started.

Freedom – they were no longer in slavery
God would help them overcome their enemies.

Jesus is the Bread of Life, the manna from heaven. But unlike the manna the Israelites ate, Jesus provides *eternal* life. And once we have eaten of the Bread from Heaven, Jesus, we can enter into the Promised Land that flows with milk and honey, life and abundance. There may be times when God needs to remind us of His priorities – that we love Him first and above all else and that we never mistake the gifts for the giver. But even when He trims our diets for a season, we can trust that the sweet, heavenly manna He provides for us will be more than enough to satisfy our every need. He's not only healthy, sweet sister, He's so delicious it will make you giddy with life!

⌘

Day 3
Learning to Rest

While I love to eat three meals a day and I'm a fan of good food, unless I'm dining at a restaurant, eating is always accompanied by work for me. I have to come up with a menu, shop for the food, prepare the meal, serve it and clean up afterwards. I get to enjoy the meal, but I also pay a heavy price for it. Such is the lot of most wives and moms (unless your husband cooks!).

If we have been dining anywhere other than our Father's table in order to have our souls satisfied, we too have been working for our meals. Personally, in the past I've shopped around for the ingredients (while hungry, no less – never a good idea!), paid a huge price for my choices, prepared the meal for myself, and even done the clean-up afterwards. Whether I was getting my fill from a substance, a relationship, or an experience, I worked hard to put the soul food on my table. I typically found those paltry meals to be less than satisfying. Afterward, I still had to clean up whatever mess I'd made in my effort to milk a little nourishment from a dry cistern.

Please read the following scriptures in your Bible and note what you learn about the kind of work the Hebrew people had to do in order to eat in the land of Egypt.

Exodus 1: 11-14 –
Exodus 5: 6-9 –
Deuteronomy 11:10 –

Hopefully you noticed that although the Hebrew people were already working very hard for their livelihood, Pharaoh and the taskmasters increased the labor to ridiculous proportions when they began to get wind of possible deliverance. They had to work even harder for what they had already been receiving with no promise of any additional reward.

When the enemy notices we've lifted our heads with hope of deliverance, he also intensifies the work load. The piddling satisfaction we had been gaining from our addiction, our bad habit, our co-dependent relationship, or our coping mechanism now requires even more from us and yet promises no greater returns. We feel the need to drink more potent alcohol, consume stronger drugs, view more pornography, spend more time with our enabler, shop for more clothes, redecorate yet another room, take a bigger cruise, or achieve another promotion. What we were doing in order to feed our souls (unfulfilling as it really was) is no longer enough. We were working hard, but now we must labor even harder. And for what? Slaves' wages.

Please read Deuteronomy 11:8-15 in your Bible. What kind of land was God giving His people?
How is this land different from the one they left?

Many times in my adult life, friends and church members have graced our family by supplying meals for several days in a row. After both of my children were born, during a prolonged bout with the flu, and after several of our moves, kind individuals prepared and furnished food for us with the intent to let me rest and to free me from cooking responsibilities during those difficult or busy times. I especially loved it when folks would bring the food in disposable containers and even supply paper plates and plastic utensils so we didn't have to wash dishes. While I'm sure my whole family appreciated the kindness of these dear friends and the food they provided, no one was more grateful then me because I'm usually the one who does the work so we can eat. I was able to enjoy good, warm and satisfying meals without lifting a finger. What a treat!

That, dear sisters, is the norm at your Father's table. Unlike the enemy, He does not expect you to work for your soul satisfying food. He gives it freely. And, unlike your favorite restaurant where you at least get to sit down and let someone else wait on you, He doesn't even charge you when you're full. Or make you wash the dishes!

Please read the following scriptures in your Bible. Match the scriptures to the corresponding insights about how God feeds His children.

Scripture:

Insight:

A. Deuteronomy 11:12

_____He doesn't charge, but invites me to eat for free

B. Deuteronomy 11:14-15   _____He sets the table with a place card just for me

C. Psalm 23:5   _____He oversees the provision from beginning to end with His own eyes

D. Isaiah 55:1   _____He invites me to sit down and serves me

E. John 6:10-11   _____He provides with perfect timing and satisfies in each season of life

I often serve our family meals from the counter tops in my kitchen. Because our kitchen table is rather small, I put the bowls of vegetables, the casserole and the bread basket on the counter top and let my family members serve their own plates before sitting down together. My 19-year-old son still prefers for me to serve his plate. Although I'm prone to make him do it himself most days, occasionally I give in and spoon out the food onto his plate. He sits down and I bring him his dinner. He's done absolutely nothing to prepare for his meal; he even had someone serve his plate. And when he's through eating, you better believe he'll suddenly remember he has a school assignment to complete so he doesn't have to help clean the kitchen.

Girlfriend, take your apron off! You may sit down just like my college boy and have someone serve you. And your Father won't serve you grudgingly as I often do my son. He'll welcome you to the table, seat you at a place He's reserved just for you, dole out generous portions, serve you graciously, and satisfy your soul with satisfying milk and sweet, delicious honey. And when you're through, when you're completely satisfied and long for no more, you won't have to make excuses in order to avoid kitchen duty. He'll clean off the table and tell you to rest easy until the next meal. No clean-up, no charge.

As we learn to have our souls satisfied by the Bread of Life and as we learn to allow Jesus the privilege of serving us a hefty portion of life with a scoop of abundance on the side, many of us will wrestle with the temptation to get up from the table and put the aprons back on. We've known the labor required by the taskmaster all too well and we're accustomed to working for our meager portions. We'll accept God's invitation to feast at His table and then hop up to serve ourselves—a royal insult to our kingly Host.

I've been painting this picture with visions of food and kitchens and dining room tables, but what could the tendency to continue working for your soul's satisfaction look like in your life? Check all that apply.

- ☐ scouting out new things to make me happy
- ☐ investing more time and effort at work
- ☐ volunteering for yet another ministry at church
- ☐ signing up for another class, group, or team
- ☐ going to more and more conferences
- ☐ reading books from the self-help shelves
- ☐ redecorating, again
- ☐ investing more in my children
- ☐ arranging more date nights, more getaways, more time with my husband
- ☐ watching Oprah for the latest advice
- ☐ getting another degree
- ☐ earning more money
- ☐ surrounding myself with people constantly
- ☐ other: _____

What does the author of Ecclesiastes 2:11 call these sorts of pursuits?

Our Father wants to serve us. He wants us to rest in His provision instead of scrambling around looking for something to cook up for ourselves.

Will it be hard for you to allow God to *serve* you that which will satisfy your soul? Why or why not?

What's the harm? Why do we need to let God provide for us without trying to work alongside of Him?

In Exodus 33:14, Deuteronomy 12:10-11, Joshua 1:13 and Joshua 21:44-45, God called the Promised Land a place of *rest*. The land flowing with milk and honey would also be a place where they could rest from their abusive labor and settle securely into His provision. He would take care of them and they would cease striving for satisfaction. God even set up a series of official rests or Sabbaths for the people to observe so they would *practice* resting in Him. He demanded they rest from their labor weekly on the seventh day (Leviticus 23:3). They were to celebrate a Sabbath rest with a holy convocation on the first of the seventh month, presenting an offering to the Lord (Leviticus 23:24). And every seventh year the people were to let the land rest, neither sowing seed nor pruning their vineyards (Leviticus 25:4).
Why did God insist the people practice resting in Him? Read Deuteronomy 8:7-20 and summarize your findings.

Now turn in your Bibles to Hebrews 4. I have one final point I want us to learn today. When you and I don't take advantage of the rest offered by God we don't only show Him our arrogance, but we do a huge disservice to those who are watching our lives from the ranks of the yet-to-be-saved. They are watching, you know. They are looking to see if we are any more satisfied, any more loved and cared for, any more at peace than they are. If they see that we indeed are satisfied, that our God does meet our every need, that we live like King's kids, then they may investigate for themselves how they too can know our God. But if we demonstrate that we are in the thick of the rat race just as they are, that we are struggling to satisfy our souls and that we have to strive for elusive peace, they will have no reason to believe the land of milk and honey really exists.

Read the following scriptures and answer the correlating questions.

Hebrews 4:3 – Who has entered His rest?

Hebrews 4:10 – What characterizes the one who has truly entered God's rest?

Hebrews 4:1 – What is the author of Hebrews concerned about?

Hebrews 4:11 – What does the author of Hebrews instruct believers to do?

The Israelites who left Egypt, save two (Joshua and Caleb), did not enter the Promised Land, the place of rest. Why not? Because when push came to shove, they didn't believe that God could provide for them to the extent He said He would. They lacked the faith to enter the land of milk and honey and rest. Despite the fact that those of us who have trusted Christ as our Savior *have* entered that Promise Land, we can still "live" separated from it when we demonstrate a lack of faith in God's provision for our soul. When we strive and work and toil in order to have our needs satisfied, just like the people who live apart from Christ, it's like we're standing outside the Promise Land picketing with signs that read "Don't Bother! It Doesn't Work!" or "God Doesn't Deliver!" Lousy advertising for the kingdom of God, isn't it? And certainly faulty.

When the world looks at you, what do they read on your sign? Is your life an advertisement for the bountiful provision of a loving God? Or do they see a life that demonstrates disbelief, a life standing outside the land of promise? Are you still working for a living or resting in the Promise Land?

Based on my attitudes, actions and words this week, other people would probably say I am...

Stressed	Calm
Striving	Relaxed
Fretful	Peaceful
Cranky	Joyful
Searching	Content
Laboring	Resting

Read Psalm 46:10 in your Bible. When we know our God, really know Him, we will cease striving and relax in His character, His ways, and His promises. What three things about your God give you the most rest and cause you to stop striving? His...

Faithfulness   Love   Goodness   Power

Gentleness   Holiness   Riches   Forgiveness

Omniscience   Graciousness   Creativity   Timing   Sovereignty

Need a little help convincing your soul to rest in God's provision? I have a scripture for us to add to our scripture memory albums that will hopefully do your soul some good and put it at rest.

Please record Psalm 116:7 on a 4x6 index card and add it to your album. I encourage you to speak this one out loud to your soul whenever you catch yourself putting that apron back on.

"Return to your rest, O my soul, for the Lord has dealt bountifully with you." (Psalm 116:7, NASB)

∿

Day 4
The Valley of Eschol

You can lead a horse to water, so they say, but you cannot make him drink. Well I'm no horse, but I can be as stubborn as a mule. A large part of learning to be content with God's soul-satisfying provisions is bending the knee, sitting down to the table and allowing Him to serve us. But in our ambitious, busy, materialistic, and success-driven world it may be hard for many of us to learn how to sit down and take in God's blessings. We mulishly strive to feed our own souls and turn up our noses at God's ample servings of sweet satisfaction.

Why do we do that? If we discover that God acknowledges our hunger, graciously offers to nourish our souls, promises to feed us well, and requires no work on our part to enjoy this feast, why would we circle around the banquet table like skeptical children and retreat back to our dry and broken cisterns time and time again? And more compelling, why would we abandon the sweet taste and overflowing abundance God has offered in exchange for the costly and less than promising diets of our Egypt? These are good questions to ask our Hebrew friends who stood on the brink of the Promised Land, but chose not to enter.

Please carefully read Numbers 13:1-33 in your Bible. This will be our focal passage for the day. Even if it's a familiar story, take it in like it's brand new to you.

Based on our initial reading, let's assign some "thumbs up" and "thumbs down" signs to this story. Just draw an upward arrow if your feelings are positive toward the person, situation, or thing. Draw a downward arrow if your feelings are negative.

_____ The mission to spy out the land

_____ The fruit found in the land

_____ The men's report about the land

_____ Caleb's conclusion about the land

_____ The people in the land

Now slowly read the passage again, marking the following in distinguishing ways:

- the men, a man, respective pronouns
- spy out
- the land, the land of Canaan
- wilderness of Paran, Kadesh
- the people (who live in the land)
- fruit or specific fruits

My bet is you are beginning to see what I wanted you to glean from this passage. But instead of disclosing the details, I'm going to give you the complete thrill of discovery today. This lesson is too concrete and applicable for me to feed you as pabulum. You deserve the opportunity to cut into this tender meat yourself.

Look back through the passage and complete the appropriate lists below based on the information in the scriptures, nothing more. Just list everything you find out about each of these things and give the verse number for reference. I'll get you started.

the men (don't list their names)
to be sent by Moses at God's request (vs. 2)
to spy out the land of Canaan (vs. 2)
a man from each tribe (vs. 2)

the land of Canaan
God is giving it to sons of Israel (vs. 2)

Assign a T for True or an F for False to each of the following statements.

1. _____The men found the land to be just as abundant and fruitful as God had promised.

2. _____God had promised them there wouldn't be any enemies to fight off in the Promise Land and they would just easily move right in. (see Exodus 23:27-30)

3. _____The men admitted that the land was just as God had promised it would be.

4. _____The land definitely appeared to be a place where they could be satisfied, but they would have to battle some giants in order to dwell there.

5. _____The people gave the promise of satisfaction more weight in their decision than the enemies they would have to overcome.

6. _____Because the people really hadn't seen God provide for them before, it makes sense that they would be skeptical about His ability to defeat their enemies.

You and I hopefully have had at least a glimpse of Promise Land living. I know I have. And I trust you also have tasted the filling and abundant milk and honey with which your Father wants to satisfy your soul. We know that other things, people, and experiences may indeed satisfy for a brief while, but the price we pay when we try to feed our souls with those things is costly and risky. Many of us have decided to leave those taskmasters behind and trust completely in our God to supply our needs. We've seen Him do it, we expect Him to do it, and we've found His provision to be deliciously satisfying. And the fact that we no longer have to work so hard to nourish our own souls is certainly the icing on the cake.

But many of us have run into an enemy or two as we've tried to settle into this land of promise. Satan doesn't want us to find contentment in the land of milk and honey. His aim is to keep us living in the wilderness of Paran just outside Canaan, but far from the fruitful bounty of God's love. And he'll try to convince us that, while the promise of fulfillment lies just over the hilltop, the price we'd have to pay in order to build our home there would be far too costly. And so, as we peruse the possibilities of God's faithful and satisfying provision, Satan causes the enemies of doubt, fear, complacency, guilt, worldliness, and people-pleasing, just to name a few, to loom large in our vision.

What giants might you personally have to fight in order to make your home once and for all in the Promise Land?

fear   loneliness   complacency   people-pleasing   pride   flesh

worldliness   doubt   addictions   lack of discipline   other:

One of my favorite TV shows is *What Not to Wear*. In this TLC program, fashion gurus Clinton and Stacy take women who don't know how to dress themselves and teach them to choose clothing that is fashionable, tasteful, flattering, and, to their credit, fairly modest. And to seal the deal, *What Not to Wear* offers each drafted participant $5,000 worth of new clothing if they'll agree to completely trash their old wardrobe and follow Clinton and Stacy's advice in building a new one.

I am amazed over and over as the two fashion experts completely transform women who once dressed in clothes that were dowdy, over-the-top sexy, masculine, too tight, too big, childish, or just plain quirky into women who look stylish and confident. The metamorphoses are absolutely stunning.

But on the way from dowdy to stylish or sleazy to tasteful, Stacy and Clinton consistently run into the same repetitive problem. Their client, though she may admit she dresses poorly, resists the changes the two experts recommend. Why? Not because the poorly dressed woman knows anything about clothing or style, but because change is uncomfortable. Without fail, these women cling to their oversized sweat shirts while Stacy and Clinton promise well fitting blouses and jackets. Or they beg to keep their outdated gypsy skirts, clunky sandals, and bodacious halter tops when the fashion experts are offering them $5,000 worth of both classic and trendy apparel. Viewers like me may be dropping our jaws at their stubbornness, but these women, clinging to what they're comfortable with and resisting the notion of change, are unable to see beyond the pain of donning something new. Not too long ago I heard Clinton say to his subject, "You've got to be willing to go through 'uncomfortable' to get to the new you. It's a necessary step in the process of change."

And so, sweet friend, I say to you today, we have to be willing to spend some time in the land of uncomfortable – fighting the necessary battles, slaying the few remaining giants, and conquering any hidden enemies – so we can arrive at a point where we are living fruitfully, comfortably and even beautifully in the land of promise.

Don't be surprised if the addictions you've left behind suddenly try to grab you with a tighter hold. Don't be alarmed when the other party in that co-dependent relationship cries "no fair!" Don't be shocked if your shopping buddy, your perpetual diet partner, your soap opera gal pals, or any other co-conspirator should try to call your bluff. And please don't be surprised when this new way of finding soul satisfaction feels a little uncomfortable, like a new garment you've never worn before.

Are you willing to do the necessary battle to live in the Promised Land of milk and honey?

_____Yes _____No _____Undecided

What battles might you have to fight? Check all that apply.

_____ adapting to relationship changes

_____ conquering lingering addictions

_____ adjusting to newly erected boundaries

_____ fighting old, hard-to-break habits

_____ staying away from places of temptation

_____ explaining new behavior and attitudes to others

_____ quieting the alluring whisper of the enemy

_____ adjusting to a higher standard of living

_____ learning to pour out to others without resentment

_____ putting your money away and not trying to earn your satisfaction

_____ learning to rest in His provision

If you are willing to fight for your opportunity to live in the land of milk and honey, not just to visit there occasionally, but to really dwell there, then you will need to prepare for the battle.

1. Use your scripture memory album like a mighty sword, speaking the Truth with conviction and power when confronted with the tempting lies of the enemy.

2. Go to battle in prayer. Confess your weaknesses, ask for divine strength and praise God for His timely intervention.

3. Enlist a mighty army. Find one or more accountability partners who will ask you the tough questions, pray for your success, and encourage your victory.

4. March forward with faith. Believe that you can conquer the lingering addictions, the bad habits, and faulty thinking that continue to live in your land like looming giants. Give the battle to the Lord and expect Him to run these enemies out. But don't counteract His work by protecting them like cherished memories of days gone by. Allow God to do a complete work in your life.

5. Seek professional help if necessary. Sister this is nothing to be ashamed of. Satan wants you to think it is, but he's a liar. Go to a Christian counselor, your pastor, your medical doctor, a weight loss program, or other appropriate specialist to get the needed help.

There's fruit in that land, dear sister. Gloriously satisfying fruit. Don't allow any giants in the land to keep you from claiming what is yours. God has already given you your land of milk and honey. Claim it with confidence and faith in Him!

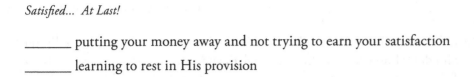

Day 5
Still Hungry? Just Wait!

I cannot believe this is our last day together. I have loved exploring the Bible with you, gleaning from it God's promise and provision for satisfying our souls with His daily bread. While we have certainly had to trudge through some soul-baring self-examination, we've also been able to take our rightful seats at the King's table with full assurance of an elaborate soul feast. I have enjoyed sharing with you the gratifying scriptures that first set me free from my daily traipse to any variety of broken, dry cisterns. The Word of God is indeed powerful, life-changing, and deeply satisfying to our hungry souls. I will miss thumbing through its pages with you.

And yet I must confess, this has been a difficult study for me to write. It has weighed heavily on my shoulders for the past several months. Not that it's been a loathsome burden, but because it has been so autobiographical in nature. As the months of writing have progressed, I have heard one woman after another say things that confirmed to me the need for such a study. I am more convinced than ever that women need to be aware that there is indeed a fountain that flows with living water from which they can drink deeply and never thirst again. I don't claim to have a corner on the market for spreading such a message, but I have tried my best to put together a study which adequately teaches those truths. Just like the Samaritan woman who encountered Jesus on her daily trip to the well, I have tried to say, "Come, see a man who told me all the things that I have done." For indeed, Jesus did expose all the things I had done in my pursuit of satisfaction. And then He took my water jar from my weary hands and offered me His living water. I can only hope at this point that you, too, have given up your water jar.

However… I still have days when I hunger. I still get thirsty for an un-nameable brand of refreshment. I still long for something more to satisfy my soul. Is that a problem? Not at all.

Please read Psalm 17:13-15 below.

"Arise, O Lord, confront him, bring him low;
Deliver my soul from the wicked with Thy sword.
From men with Thy hand, O Lord,
From men of the world, whose portion is in this life;
And whose belly Thou dost fill with Thy treasure;
They are satisfied with children,
And leave their abundance to their babes.
As for me, I shall behold Thy face in righteousness;
I will be satisfied with Thy likeness when I awake."
(Psalm 17:13-15, NASB)

This psalm of David expresses his disdain for and angst towards his enemy. In his soul-baring and transparent cry to God, he pleads for the Lord to listen to his "just cause" for requesting a divine confrontation with his nemesis. I didn't have you read the entire Psalm because most of it deals with David's plea for vengeance. But I wanted you to read these final verses because, at this point, David finally realizes one of the primary differences between him and his foe. And in this realization David actually seems to be freed up to move on whether God takes down his enemy or not.

Here are a few things worthy of noting before I ask you some questions about this passage. These are simply word choice clarifications that might help us better understand the scripture.

- An acceptable substitute for "whose portion is in this life" in verse 14 is "whose portion in life is of this world."
- The *Holman Christian Standard Bible* and *New International Version* both translate "babes" in verse 14 as children. They store up or leave their wealth for their *children*.
- Several translations, including the *HCSB*, translate "likeness" in verse 15 to read "presence."

Underline the portions of Psalm 17:13-15 that describe "the men" with whom David takes offense.
These men are experiencing fullness of what sort?

Who is providing this fullness?

Just how full are they? Circle the portion of scripture that tells what they are doing with the excess.

Now put a box around the portion of scripture that identifies when David expects to be satisfied. What will satisfy him?

Do you ever get frustrated because worldly people *seem* to be blissfully content while you are still hungry for something more? Does it ever *appear* to you that the "wicked" are fat with worldly possessions, fame, fortune, and power, while you are still deficient? And, quite honestly, do you ever wonder why the "Jones" *look* like they're perfectly content while you're supposed to be sharing with them the answer to their *dis*satisfaction? I think that's kind of where David was. He was wondering why everything seemed so upside down when He was the one who knew the King of the universe intimately and yet the enemies of that king seemed perfectly happy, satisfied, and prosperous.

What conclusion do you think David finally came to?

David seems to have realized that while others may *appear* to be living the abundant life, he actually had the satisfaction afforded only by living rightly before a holy God. Even more importantly, while others were finding satisfaction through the *stuff* of this present world, he would find ultimate satisfaction when he awoke from death's slumber in the presence of God and finally saw Him face to face.

We also will not find our ultimate and most fulfilling dose of soul satisfaction until we are living in the very presence of our Lord and Savior, Jesus Christ. Through the indwelling of the Holy Spirit and the power of God's Word we are able to experience a taste of sweet communion now; however, until we look Him in the face and hear His loving voice we will continue to ache for the pure fellowship for which we were created. That, sweet sisters, is a good thing. It is the ache and hunger which keeps us pressing forward, keeps us from becoming so easily entangled in the deceitful allure of this world, and keeps us drawing ever closer to Him.

Please read the scriptures below and underline the phrases that indicate the benefits of an ongoing, healthy hunger.

A worker's appetite works for him, for his hunger urges him on. (Proverbs 16:26)

"Blessed are those who hunger and thirst for righteousness, for they shall be satisfied."
(Matthew 5:6)

"Blessed are you who hunger now, for you shall be satisfied." (Luke 6:21a)
(For some insight into the converse, read Luke 6:25.)

Ecclesiastes 3:11 tells us God intentionally set a hunger for eternity in the hearts of all people. Why? So we will continuously long for "the end of the story."

I have a confession to make. When I read fiction I always start at the beginning, but once I'm a couple of chapters into the book and have developed an affinity for the characters I take a peek at the ending. I just have to know how things are going to turn out for my new friends. It's a bad habit I picked up from my mom, but it's just the way I do things. Unfortunately my little vice has also kept me from finishing many a good novel. I'm simply no longer "hungry" for the ending once my curiosity has been sufficiently satisfied.

If we were to be completely content right now we would have no more motivation to strive toward eternity than I do to finish a novel. But God has so ordained it that even though He satisfies us with our daily bread, we still wake up each morning hungry in our souls. We still know there is more, that something is missing. And we still long for something, some *One* who can both take our breath away and breathe life into every crevice of our being, all at the same time.

It's very important that we get this final lesson under our belts because you will undoubtedly wake up hungry tomorrow, sweet sister. You will still have days when you long, thirst, crave, hunger…for something. And if you misinterpret that ongoing hunger, that aching dissatisfaction, for anything other than what it is, the enemy will have you right where he wants you once again—searching for substance to fill the void. Don't fall prey to his deceptions. Recognize your ache as a holy hunger and allow it to motivate you to draw closer still to your God.

Meanwhile, take heart. I'm going to get you to follow my sneaky little habit and take a peek at the "end of the story." Don't worry; this peek won't spoil your appetite, but will only whet it.

Please read Revelation 21 & 22. Read with a voracious appetite, dear sister; for this is just a taste of things to come. Mark the references to food and water in distinguishing ways. Then answer a few final questions.

1. What river will we find in the holy city? (Rev. 22:1)

2. Who is invited to "come" and drink from the water of life without cost? (Rev. 21:6; 22:17)

3. What tree will we find in the holy city? (Rev. 22:2)

4. Where exactly is that tree? Describe it. (Rev. 22:2)

5. Revelation 22:3 says there shall no longer be any _____.

6. According to Revelation 22:14, who has the right to that tree?

One day we will drink freely from the river of life and eat heartily from twelve different crops of fruit born from the tree of life. But that, dear one, is not what will satisfy our souls like they've never been satisfied before. We will not need a lamp or sunlight to illumine us. The radiance of God will light our way. Similarly, we will not rely on other things, people or experiences to thrill our souls. In the holy city, we will find complete and utter satisfaction in the intimate presence of the triune God. The Creator God, the Prince of Peace, the Mighty Counselor, the God Who Provides, the Bread of Life, the Comforter, the God Who Sees, the Good Shepherd, the Teacher, our friend and father—He will finally walk in our midst again. And all of us whose names are written in the Lamb's book of life will be able to say we truly are satisfied…at last.

"Blessed are those who wash their robes, that they may have the right to the tree of life, and may enter by the gates into the city." Revelation 22:14

Week 6
Discussion Questions

1. Describe the bondage from which God delivered the Israelites. How does their slavery correspond to some of the things from which you or your sisters may have walked away from during the course of this study?

2. What substances, types of relationships, or experiences would you assume would be most indelibly etched into the senses so a person would long for them the way the Israelites desired the strong and vibrant flavors of their Egyptian foods?

3. Have you personally experienced a wilderness season when it seemed that all your soul had to feast upon was that which proceeds out of the mouth of God? How did that season affect you?

4. What are some new things you learned about manna? How does the Israelites' diet of manna from heaven relate to our eating the Bread of Life?

5. Share some of the ways in which you wrestle with the desire to "work for" your soul satisfaction. Why do you think we resist giving God the time and room to serve us instead?

6. Why is our ability to "rest" in God's provision for our soul's needs actually a form of testimony to lost friends and family? What would help you to rest in God more instead of laboring for soul satisfaction?

7. What are some of the giants you've had to fight off in order to seek soul satisfaction from Jesus in the land of promise? What battle tactics have been the most successful for you so far?

8. At what times are you most prone to long for heaven? What are the sweetest and most precious promises of heaven in your estimation?

About the Author

Kay Harms loves teaching women how to apply the ancient words of the Bible to their modern lives. Her first Bible study, *The View from My Front Porch*, explores how our worldviews are most commonly formed and shows women why and how to view the world from God's perspective. The author of numerous devotions and magazine articles, Kay also writes each week at www.offthebeatenpathministries.com, a blog she established to offer biblical encouragement to women following Jesus on the narrow path.

Raised in Georgia, Kay has followed her husband James to Arizona, where he tends to a local flock of believers and she concentrates on their two children. Kay also serves as a mentor mom for a local MOPS chapter, leads the women's ministry at her church, speaks at women's conferences and teaches weekly Bible studies for women.